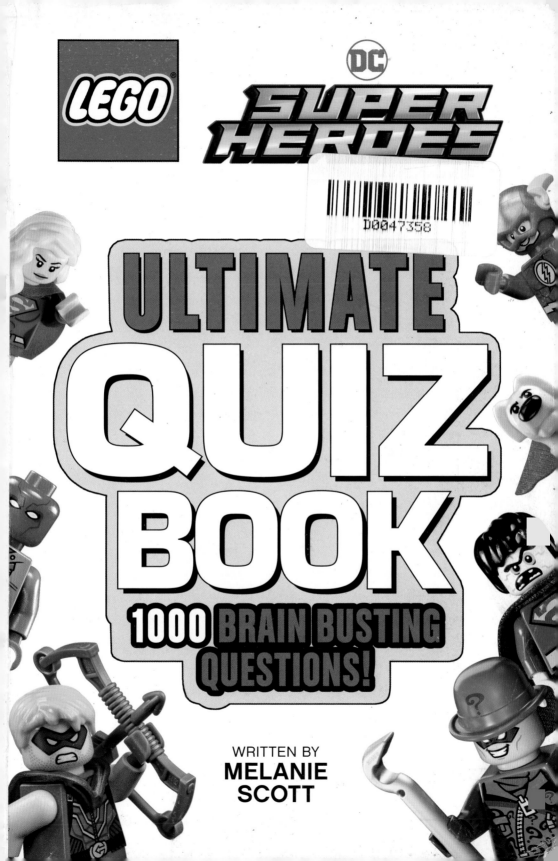

LEGO®

DC SUPER HEROES

ULTIMATE QUIZ BOOK

1000 BRAIN BUSTING QUESTIONS!

WRITTEN BY
MELANIE SCOTT

CONTENTS

I'LL TAKE THAT! DON'T YOU KNOW CRIME DOESN'T PAY?

THE UNIVERSE

NOT SO FAST, CHEETAH!

AND I'LL TAKE THIS ONE!

SUPER HEROES

WHAT DO YOU CALL A *FISH* WITH NO EYE? ...*FSH!*

Superman

The Flash

Aquaman

WONDER WOMAN

This warrior had much to learn about humans when she arrived in our world. How much do you know about the Amazon Princess?

1 What is Wonder Woman's real first name?

a. Lois   b. Diana   c. Athena   d. Wonder

2 In the LEGO® Wonder Woman Warrior Battle set, what weapon does Wonder Woman wield?

a. Bow and arrow   c. Magic wand
b. Sword   d. Custard pie

3 Which female-only race does Wonder Woman belong to?

a. Amazonian   c. Oans
b. Kryptonians   d. Atlanteans

4 How many Wonder Woman LEGO minifigures have there been?

a. 1   b. 30   c. 6   d. 100

5 True or false? Wonder Woman has no father

6 Where did Wonder Woman grow up?

a. Paradise Island   c. Apokolips
b. Metropolis   d. Central City

7 What is the name of Wonder Woman's royal mother?

a. Hippolyta   c. Artemis
b. Antiope   d. Hera

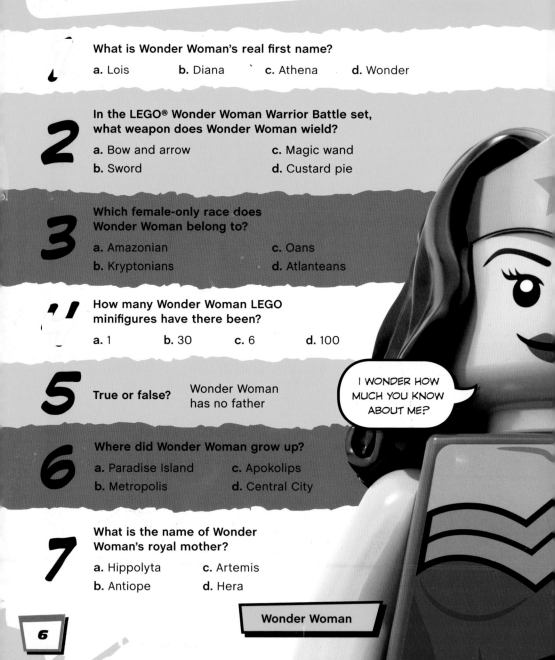

I WONDER HOW MUCH YOU KNOW ABOUT ME?

Wonder Woman

8 Who is the God of War that Wonder Woman was born to fight?

a. Zeus   b. Ares   c. Hades   d. Poseidon

9 Who was the first human to meet Wonder Woman?

a. Bruce Wayne   b. Barbara Minerva   c. Steve Trevor   d. Lex Luthor

10 What vehicle does Wonder Woman drive in the LEGO Gorilla Grodd Goes Bananas set?

a. Invisible Jet   c. Themysciran Taxicab
b. Wondermobile   d. Car of Truth

11 Bad guys caught in Wonder Woman's famous Golden Lasso are forced to...

a. Clean her boots   c. Be exiled to Apokolips
b. Take themselves to Arkham Asylum   d. Tell the truth

12 Which of these is NOT one of Wonder Woman's powers?

a. Super-strength   c. Super-speed
b. Ability to fly   d. X-ray vision

13 Which team of Super Heroes is Wonder Woman a member of?

a. Green Lantern Corps   c. Teen Titans
b. Justice League   d. Amazon Army

14 Which part of Wonder Woman's costume can deflect bullets?

a. Bracelets   c. Lasso
b. Tiara   d. Boots

15 Which beastly super-villain is Wonder Woman's archenemy?

a. Gorilla Grodd   c. Man-Bat
b. Killer Croc   d. Cheetah

GENIUS QUESTION
Wonder Woman briefly had a job at a fast-food chain! What kind of cuisine did it serve?

SUPERMAN

An alien who has become one of Earth's greatest protectors, Superman is one of the most famous Super Heroes ever.

1 What gives Superman his superpowers?
- **a.** Magic spell
- **b.** Earth's yellow sun
- **c.** Martha Kent's cooking
- **d.** Energy drinks

2 One of Superman's only weaknesses is Kryptonite. What else makes him weak?
- **a.** Fire
- **b.** Magic
- **c.** Candy
- **d.** Carbon dioxide

3 True or false? One of the LEGO Superman minifigures has heat vision.

4 After crashing on Earth, where did the young Superman grow up?
- **a.** Metropolis
- **b.** Gotham City
- **c.** Smallville
- **d.** Themyscira

5 Superman's adoptive parents are Jonathan and Martha Kent. What are their jobs?
- **a.** Farmers
- **b.** Shopkeepers
- **c.** Scientists
- **d.** Reporters

6 True or false? The commonest form of Kryptonite is green.

7 What was the name Superman was given by his Kryptonian birth parents?
- **a.** Jor-El
- **b.** Tor-An
- **c.** Mon-El
- **d.** Kal-El

8 True or false? While on Earth, Superman can fly faster than the speed of sound.

GENIUS QUESTION
Even Super Heroes need to chill out with a movie sometimes. What is Superman's favorite film?

9 What does Batman keep in the Batcave in case Superman should one day run out of control?

a. Stun gun

b. Tranquilizer darts

c. Green Kryptonite

d. Large net

10 True or false? Superman's S-shield is Kryptonian.

11 What is Superman's best-known nickname?

a. Man of Iron

b. Man of Steel

c. Kryptonian Crusader

d. Strongest Man Alive

UP, UP, AND AWAY!

12 Which of these Superman enemies is not an alien?

a. Lex Luthor

b. Doomsday

c. General Zod

d. Brainiac

13 Which substance blocks Superman's X-ray vision power?

a. Lead

b. Brick

c. Water

d. Peanut butter

14 True or false? Vampires cannot harm Superman.

15 Which hero is Superman's Kryptonian cousin?

a. Superboy

b. Supergirl

c. Superwoman

d. Starfire

16 Which evil female Kryptonian is included in the Superman: Battle for Smallville LEGO set?

a. Lara-El

b. Kara Zor-El

c. Lois Lane

d. Faora

Superman

Answers on page 116

BATMAN

Respected by his fellow heroes and feared by criminals, Batman has trained himself to be fit and strong so that he can keep his city safe.

> I DON'T MAKE JOKES— I CATCH *JOKERS!*

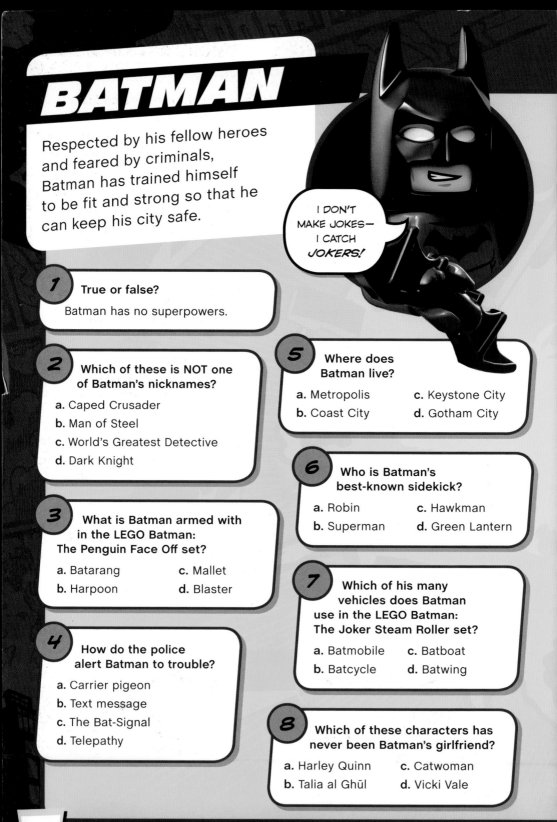

1 True or false?

Batman has no superpowers.

2 Which of these is NOT one of Batman's nicknames?

a. Caped Crusader
b. Man of Steel
c. World's Greatest Detective
d. Dark Knight

3 What is Batman armed with in the LEGO Batman: The Penguin Face Off set?

a. Batarang   c. Mallet
b. Harpoon   d. Blaster

4 How do the police alert Batman to trouble?

a. Carrier pigeon
b. Text message
c. The Bat-Signal
d. Telepathy

5 Where does Batman live?

a. Metropolis   c. Keystone City
b. Coast City   d. Gotham City

6 Who is Batman's best-known sidekick?

a. Robin   c. Hawkman
b. Superman   d. Green Lantern

7 Which of his many vehicles does Batman use in the LEGO Batman: The Joker Steam Roller set?

a. Batmobile   c. Batboat
b. Batcycle   d. Batwing

8 Which of these characters has never been Batman's girlfriend?

a. Harley Quinn   c. Catwoman
b. Talia al Ghūl   d. Vicki Vale

9 What is the name of Batman's son?

a. Tim   c. Damian

b. Jason   d. Clark

14 What is on the front of LEGO Batman's Mighty Micros car?

a. A big flower   c. A giant smile

b. Flames   d. A bat-symbol

10 Which of his fellow Justice League members is Batman's biggest fan?

a. Wonder Woman   c. Superman

b. Cyborg   d. Green Lantern

15 Which is the only LEGO Batman minifigure to come with a big smile?

a. Scuba Batman

b. Arctic Batman

c. Fairy Batman

d. Batman of Zurr-En-Arrh

11 What color are the cape and cowl of Batman's LEGO Classic TV Series minifigure?

a. Black   c. Blue

b. Purple   d. Yellow

16 Who is the technical whiz at Wayne Industries who keeps Batman stocked with gadgets?

a. Alfred Pennyworth   c. Barbara Gordon

b. Lucius Fox   d. Selina Kyle

12 True or false?

Batman knows Superman's secret identity.

13 Which of Batman's vehicles is this?

a. Batmobile   c. Tumbler

b. Batcopter   d. Dragster

17 What is the collective name for all the mad, bad, and dangerous foes that Batman faces?

a. The Evil Empire   c. The Dirty Dozen

b. The Legion of Bad Guys   d. The Rogues Gallery

GENIUS QUESTION

What movie character helped to inspire Batman's costume?

Answers on page 116

FLYING FOX

The Batmobile is the coolest vehicle ever, but for some missions it needs to hitch a ride on the Justice League's Flying Fox!

1 Which of Superman's powers is he using here?

a. Freeze breath
b. X-ray vision
c. Heat vision
d. Super-strength

2 True or false?

This bad guy is Darkseid.

3 True or false?

A Mother Box is a powerful extraterrestrial device.

4 What symbol appears on Wonder Woman's shield?

a. A letter W
b. An eagle
c. A heart
d. A rose

5 What is the name of this LEGO Batsuit?

a. Tactical suit
b. Big boss suit
c. Scuba suit
d. Disco Batsuit

Flying Fox: Batmobile Airlift Attack (76087)

6 Which hero designed the Flying Fox for the Justice League to use?

a. Superman **c.** Cyborg
b. Wonder Woman **d.** Batman

7 True or false?

The weapon Cyborg is using here is part of his body.

8 True or false?

The Batmobile fits inside the Flying Fox aircraft.

9 How many stud shooters is the Batmobile armed with?

a. None **c.** Two
b. One **d.** Three

10 How many minifigures fit inside the Batmobile's cockpit?

a. None
b. One
c. Six
d. Ten

WAYNE TECHNOLOGY

13

TRUE OR FALSE?
BATMAN'S GADGETS

Batman has many cool gadgets to help him fight crime. Do you know your Batarangs from your Bat-Signals?

1 Batman can summon a colony of bats to help him.

2 Batman carries a mouthpiece in his Utility Belt that allows him to breathe under water.

3 The LEGO Pirate Batman minifigure comes with a cannonball.

4 Batman's computer is called the Bat-pad.

5 Batarangs are a type of throwing weapon.

6 In the LEGO Arctic Batman Vs. Mr. Freeze: Aquaman on Ice set, Batman's special Arctic Batsuit is purple.

7 Batman uses the Bat-Signal to tell the police he is on a mission.

8 In the LEGO Green Lantern vs. Sinestro set, Batman has a jet pack and wings.

9 Batman carries stink bombs in his Utility Belt.

10 Batman uses his Bat-Mech suit in the LEGO DC Gorilla Grodd Goes Bananas set.

11 In the LEGO Heroes of Justice: Sky High Battle set, Batman is armed with a Batarang.

12 Batman's computer has a database of every criminal Batman has faced.

13 Batman wears a desert Batsuit to take on Rā's al Ghūl in the LEGO Batman: Rescue from Rā's al Ghūl set.

14 If Batman needs the Batmobile on a mission, he has to get Robin to bring it to him.

15 The LEGO Batman of Zur-En-Arrh is armed with a baseball bat.

16 Batman's cowl is the only part of his regular Batsuit that isn't armed.

17 Batman stores as many of his gadgets as possible in his Utility Belt.

18 If an enemy stole Batman's Utility Belt, they could use all of his gadgets.

19 Among the many things that Batman carries with him is a Crime Scene Investigation Kit.

20 Scarecrow once customized the Bat-Signal to project the image of a jack o'lantern.

21 In the LEGO Batman: The Penguin Face Off set, Batman is wearing a spacesuit.

22 Batman once fought off a shark using a can of shark-repellent spray.

23 Batman carries small explosive devices with him.

24 In the LEGO Clash of the Heroes set, Batman has a Kryptonite gun to combat Superman.

25 Batman has to be in the Batcave to use his high-tech computer.

26 Batman once wore an enchanted suit of armor given to him by the villain Talia al Ghūl.

27 When it is raining, Batman gets out his umbrella Batarang.

28 Lenses in Batman's cowl give him night vision, x-ray vision, or thermal imaging.

29 Batman once used a heated Batarang to defeat Clayface.

30 Batman has a lie-detector machine in the Batcave.

Answers on page 116

BAT-FAMILY

Batman doesn't have to battle Gotham City's super-villains on his own. A select band of heroes and allies is always ready to stand by his side.

1 What is Barbara Gordon's **ALTER EGO?**

a. Batwoman
b. Wonder Woman
c. Catwoman
d. Batgirl

2 How is **ROBIN** Dick Grayson related to Batman?

a. Nephew
b. Cousin
c. Brother
d. Adopted son

3 Whose LEGO minifigure fights with blue weapons called **ESCRIMA STICKS?**

a. Nightwing
b. Red Robin
c. Batgirl
d. Alfred

4 Kate Kane is Batwoman— what is the color of the **BAT-SYMBOL** on her costume?

a. White
b. Yellow
c. Gray
d. Red

5 Who teams up with **BATMAN** in the LEGO Batman: Man-Bat Attack set?

a. Batgirl
b. Red Robin
c. Nightwing
d. Red Hood

6 What is **BATGIRL ARMED WITH** in the LEGO Batman: The Joker Steam Roller set?

a. Nothing
b. Batarang
c. Blaster
d. Bow and arrow

7 Who is Batgirl's **FATHER?**

a. Batman
b. The Joker
c. Alfred
d. Commissioner Gordon

8 Which of the **BATMAN FAMILY** appears in the LEGO Batman: Killer Croc Smash set?

a. Batgirl
b. Red Robin
c. Nightwing
d. Red Hood

9 What is Robin's **NICKNAME?**

a. Mini-Bat
b. Boy Wonder
c. Mighty Bird
d. Acrobatman

10 True or false? One of Alfred's most important jobs is to remind Batman to eat lunch.

11 True or false? Kate Kane, a.k.a. Batwoman, is Bruce Wayne's sister.

12 In the LEGO Mighty Micros: Robin vs. Bane set,

WHAT WEAPON
does Robin use?

a. Dynamite
c. Water gun
b. Shark repellent
d. Grapple-hook gun

13 What color is the
BAT-SYMBOL
on Batgirl's costume?

a. Black
c. Gray
b. Yellow
d. Red

14 Who fights alongside
BATMAN
in the LEGO Batman: The Joker Steam Roller set?

a. Alfred and Batgirl
b. Batgirl and Robin
c. Red Hood and Robin
d. Batwoman and Batgirl

15 Who does
NIGHTWING
go up against in his LEGO Mighty Micros contest?

a. Bane
b. Killer Moth
c. The Joker
d. Scarecrow

16 True or false?
Batgirl and Batwoman have the same color hair.

17 Batgirl is
GOOD FRIENDS
with which of these characters?

a. Harley Quinn
c. Black Canary
b. Catwoman
d. Supergirl

ALFRED, COULD YOU LAY OUT MY *BUNNY SLIPPERS* FOR WHEN I GET HOME?

OF COURSE, *MASTER BRUCE!*

Alfred

GENIUS QUESTION

Who did Alfred work for as a butler before Bruce Wayne?

THE FLASH

The Flash can outrun a speeding bullet and pretty much everything else, too! But do you know the fast facts about the Scarlet Speedster?

HOW FAST CAN YOU ANSWER THESE QUESTIONS?

1 Who is The Flash's alter ego?

a. Leonard Snart
b. Barry Allen
c. Hal Jordan
d. Victor Stone

2 What is The Flash's nickname?

a. The Fastest Man Alive
b. Lightning Lad
c. Man of Speed
d. The Quick Crusader

3 What is the name of the mystical energy from which The Flash gets his power?

a. The Bleed
b. Omega Beams
c. The Speed Force
d. The Emotional Spectrum

4 What is the name of The Flash's sidekick?

a. Kid Flash   c. Speedy
b. Flash Boy   d. Lightning Lad

5 What is The Flash's day job?

a. Firefighter
b. Doctor
c. Forensic scientist
d. Reporter

6 How did The Flash get his powers?

a. He fell into a vat of radioactive slime
b. He was doused in chemicals and struck by lightning
c. He was caught in a solar flare
d. From genetic experiments

7 Where does The Flash live?

a. Gotham City   c. Coast City
b. Metropolis   d. Central City

8 True or false?
The Flash has the power of time travel.

9 True or false?
The Flash is so fast that he once beat Superman in a race.

10 Which Super Hero does The Flash team up with in the LEGO Knightcrawler Tunnel Attack set?

a. Wonder Woman
b. Hawkman
c. Batman
d. Superman

11 What is the name of The Flash's girlfriend?

a. Patty East
b. Rosie North
c. Betty South
d. Iris West

12 Which of these is NOT one of The Flash's enemies?

a. Sultan of Spin
b. Weather Wizard
c. Mirror Master
d. Captain Cold

13 As well as super-speed, which of these powers does The Flash possess?

a. Heat vision
b. Invisibility
c. Super-fast healing
d. Flight

14 Which of The Flash's archenemies is really named Eobard Thawne?

a. Captain Cold
b. Weather Wizard
c. Trickster
d. Reverse-Flash

15 Which of these is NOT a handy additional benefit of The Flash's super-speed?

a. His own wifi hotspot
b. The ability to let bullets pass through his body
c. Being able to deliver a massive light-speed punch
d. Invulnerability against mind control

16 In the LEGO Gorilla Grodd Goes Bananas set, Batman, Wonder Woman, and The Flash fight Gorilla Grodd. Which other villain do they fight in this set?

a. Captain Cold
b. The Penguin
c. The Joker
d. Catwoman

17 In his LEGO Mighty Micros set, what accessory does The Flash minifigure come with?

a. An umbrella
b. An energy drink
c. A pogo stick
d. A Batarang

TRUE OR FALSE?
JUSTICE LEAGUE

They are the ultimate Super Hero team-up, a group of the most powerful beings on Planet Earth. But how well do you know the Justice League?

1 Cyborg used to be a talented football star.

2 Plastic Man's LEGO minifigure has the same hairpiece as Superman.

3 Cyborg does not need to eat or sleep.

4 Aquaman is half human.

5 The Justice League has seven founding members.

6 Hawkman is not from Earth.

7 Aquaman needs breathing equipment to attend Justice League meetings.

8 Green Lantern's girlfriend is fellow Super Hero Black Canary.

9 Green Lantern's power only lasts as long as his power ring remains fully charged.

10 Cyborg's costume can be removed at the touch of a button.

11 Green Arrow's alter ego is billionaire Oliver Queen.

12 Martian Manhunter's one weakness is his aversion to fire.

WE'RE HERE TO BRING SOME *JUSTICE* TO THE WORLD!

Aquaman

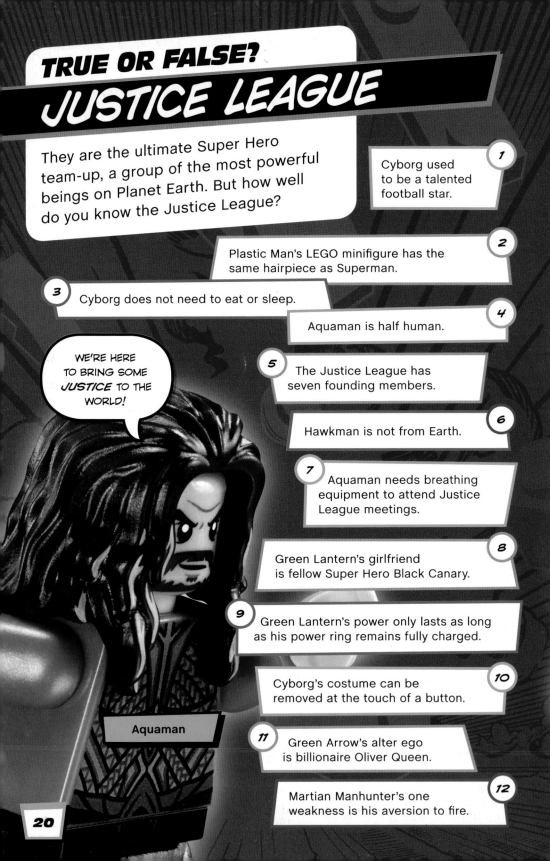

13 Superman once lost a Justice League leadership election because he voted for Batman.

14 Wonder Woman is one of two female founding members of the Justice League.

15 There is only one minifigure version of Cyborg.

16 In his former life as a criminal, Plastic Man's nickname was Squid.

17 The Flash can magnetize his boots.

18 Green Lantern's energy comes from the emotion of hope.

19 Hawkman's power comes from the alien element Promethium.

20 The Justice League Watchtower is in Happy Harbor, Rhode Island.

21 Wonder Woman designed the headquarters of the Justice League —the Hall of Justice building.

22 Aquaman can communicate with fish.

23 The Justice League was originally formed to guard the Batmobile from being stolen.

24 The Justice League once defeated a giant alien starfish.

25 Aquaman can swim at speeds of up to 10,000 feet per second.

26 Martian Manhunter's real name is J'onn J'onzz.

27 The Riddler and Batman battle Darkseid together in a LEGO set.

28 Batman and Wonder Woman have teamed up in three LEGO sets.

29 Green Arrow has no superpowers.

30 Batman and Superman fight against one another in one LEGO set.

Cyborg

TEEN TITANS

The Teen Titans are a team of amazing teenage Super Heroes. Many of them are sidekicks to other heroes, as well as being awesome heroes in their own right.

GENIUS QUESTION

There is an evil version of the Teen Titans called the Terror Titans. Who is their leader?

1 In the LEGO Teen Titans Go! Team Pack, what is the Beast Boy minifigure holding?

a. A blaster   c. A sword

b. A bow and arrow   d. A banana

2 Which Teen Titan is also a member of the Justice League?

a. Raven   b. Cyborg   c. Robin   d. Beast Boy

3 What color hair does the Starfire LEGO minifigure have?

a. Green   b. Blue   c. Pink   d. Purple

4 True or false?   Raven can turn into a real raven.

THESE QUESTIONS ARE BEASTLY!

5 What is Raven's father?

a. A Super Hero   c. An accountant

b. A demon   d. A bird

6 Who was NOT one of the original Teen Titans?

a. Starfire   c. Aqualad

b. Robin   d. Kid Flash

7 What color do Raven's eyes glow when she is using magic?

a. Red   b. Green   c. White   d. Silver

Beast Boy

8 Which Super Hero identity does Dick Grayson take after Robin?

a. Beast Boy   b. Red Hood   c. Azrael   d. Nightwing

9 How did Beast Boy get his shape-shifting powers?

a. He was struck by lightning

b. He was born with them

c. After eating a bad anchovy

d. From an untested antidote after an animal bite

10 What is Starfire's real name?

a. O'regano　b. Sinnam'n　c. Koriand'r　d. Parslee

11 After the heroes left New York City, which city did they build the new Titans Tower in?

a. Metropolis

b. Gotham City

c. San Francisco

d. Miami

12 What was the profession of Robin's family, the Graysons?

a. Circus acrobats

b. Veterinarians

c. Ninjas-for-hire

d. Restaurateurs

Robin

13 What is Starfire's preferred method of learning human languages?

a. Online courses

b. Kissing a human

c. Reading books

d. Going to school

14 What is the real name of Beast Boy?

a. Gar Logan　b. Tim Drake　c. Jason Todd　d. Bart Allen

15 Which Super Hero team did Beast Boy's adoptive parents belong to?

a. The Doom Patrol

b. The Justice League

c. The Green Lantern Corps

d. The Rogues Gallery

16 In the LEGO Darkseid Invasion set, who does Cyborg team up with against Darkseid?

a. Superman and Hawkman

b. Catwoman and the Penguin

c. Robin and Alfred

d. The Flash and Plastic Man

WEIRD AND WONDERFUL

There are many Super Heroes in the Universe besides the Justice League. Some are stranger than others—but all of them are amazing in their own way!

GENIUS QUESTION

Which hero is the daughter of stage magician John Zatara?

1

How are Supergirl's powers different from Superman's?

a. They're not, but she's still learning how to use them

b. Her X-ray vision works on lead

c. She has no heat vision

d. They're exact opposites

2

How did Kid Flash get his powers?

a. He was born with them

b. Through magic

c. He was struck by lightning while covered in chemicals

d. He wished for them

3

Which hero teams up with Batman in the LEGO Batman: Scarecrow Harvest of Fear set?

a. Blue Beetle   b. Lightning Lad   c. Superboy   d. Atom

4

Which Japanese hero uses a sword in battle?

a. Black Canary   c. Zatanna

b. Mera   d. Katana

5

Who does Supergirl face in her LEGO Mighty Micros set?

a. Brainiac   c. Lois Lane

b. Bizarro   d. Superman

Blue Beetle

6

Which century do Cosmic Boy and Lightning Lad come from?

a. 20th   b. 21st   c. 25th   d. 30th

7 Which Super Hero's real name is Dinah Lance?

    a. Zatanna   **b.** Black Canary   **c.** Katana   **d.** Vixen

8 Who is the alter ego of Helena Bertinelli?

    a. Huntress   **b.** Raven   **c.** Star Sapphire   **d.** Hawkgirl

9 The Supergirl minifigure has a face with red eyes to show which of her powers?

    a. Freeze breath   **c.** X-ray vision

    b. Heat vision   **d.** Super-speed

10 Which futuristic hero is accompanied by a robot named Skeets?

    a. Lightning Lad   **c.** Booster Gold

    b. Cosmic Boy   **d.** Kid Flash

11 **True or false?** Miss Martian is a different alien race from Martian Manhunter.

12 **True or false?** Mera is from Atlantis.

13 Who is known as Earth's Greatest Sorcerer?

    a. Huntress   **c.** Doctor Fate

    b. John Stewart   **d.** Blue Beetle

Katana

14 Which Tamaran princess Super Hero can shoot starbolt energy from her hands?

    a. Starburst   **c.** Stargirl

    b. Starfire   **d.** Starbright

15 Which of these is the shape-shifting hero Beast Boy?

A.   *B.*   *C.*   *D.*

16 **True or false?** Two people combine to create the Super Hero Firestorm the Nuclear Man.

TRUE OR FALSE?
ALTER EGOS

One of a hero's most challenging tasks is to maintain a secret identity. When they are not fighting crime, they need to blend in with ordinary citizens.

1 In the LEGO Batcave Break-In set, the Bruce Wayne minifigure is wearing a white tuxedo.

2 Bruce Wayne's friend Harvey Dent becomes the villain the Riddler.

3 Bruce's company is called Wayne Industries.

4 Batgirl is not Barbara Gordon's only secret identity.

5 Lois Lane is the only ordinary person who knows that Clark Kent is Superman.

6 Hal Jordan is the alter ego of Green Lantern.

7 Clark Kent uses his powers to win strongman contests.

8 The Flash Barry Allen studied LEGO building at college.

9 Aquaman Arthur Curry is the son of a fisherman.

10 Supergirl Kara Zor-El is from the same planet as Superman.

11 Patrick O'Brian is the cheerful Super Hero Plastic Man.

12 Blue Beetle Jaime Reyes is still at school.

13 Bruce Wayne's cousin Kate Kane is Batwoman.

14 The Superman costume is not visible on the Clark Kent LEGO minifigure.

15 Batgirl Barbara Gordon is the sister of Commissioner Jim Gordon.

16 Bruce Wayne is a champion table football player.

17 The powerful hero Shazam's alter ego is a young boy.

18 Batgirl Barbara Gordon doesn't like to use technology.

19 Tatsu Yamashiro, the alter ego of Katana, is from Japan.

20 Dinah Lance is the alter ego of Hawkgirl.

21 The Atom's alter ego, Ray Palmer, works at a top university.

22 Helena Bertinelli is the alter ego of Huntress.

23 Aquaman Arthur Curry cannot swim.

24 Star Sapphire was a villain before becoming a hero.

25 The Teen Titan Raven's alter ego is Koriand'r.

26 Teenager Wally West is the alter ego of Kid Flash.

27 One of Robin Dick Grayson's LEGO minifigures holds a can of shark repellent.

28 Kate Kane does not know that her cousin Bruce Wayne is Batman.

29 Mari McCabe and her grandmother both used the Super Hero identity Vixen.

30 Hal Jordan is afraid of heights.

EXCUSE ME, I'M LOOKING FOR *SUPERMAN*. DO YOU KNOW HIM? HE WEARS RED AND BLUE AND DOESN'T HAVE MUCH OF A *PERSONALITY*.

I HAVE *NO IDEA* WHO YOU'RE TALKING ABOUT.

Bruce Wayne

Clark Kent

Answers on page 118

ALLIES

Even high-powered heroes need regular human friends to help them from time to time. These ordinary citizens may not have superpowers, but they are still important allies.

1 What is the name of Bruce Wayne's loyal butler?
a. Dick Grayson
b. Alfred Pennyworth
c. Jim Gordon
d. Tim Drake

2 In the LEGO The Bat vs. Bane: Tumbler Chase set, what is the name of the police officer who helps Batman?
a. Officer Penguin
b. Sergeant Bane
c. Captain Cold
d. Commissioner Gordon

3 What is the name of Clark Kent's photographer friend at the *Daily Planet*?
a. Lois Lane
b. Perry White
c. Bruce Wayne
d. Jimmy Olsen

4 What is the name of Superman's faithful canine ally?
a. Fido
b. Bonzo
c. Krypto
d. Ace

5 What is the job of Vicki Vale, Batman's on-off girlfriend?
a. Lawyer
b. Reporter
c. Doctor
d. Police officer

6 What is Lois Lane's middle name?
a. Jane
b. Jill
c. Joanne
d. Jasmine

7 What is the name of Clark Kent's editor at the *Daily Planet*?
a. Perry White
b. Sherry Black
c. Kerry Gray
d. Terry Pink

Commissioner Gordon

SW

8 What organization does Commissioner Gordon work for?

a. S.T.A.R. Labs
b. The *Daily Planet*
c. Gotham City Police Department
d. Metropolis Mayor's Office

9 **True or false?** Lois Lane has won the Pulitzer Prize for her outstanding work as a journalist.

10 In the LEGO Batman 2: DC Super Heroes video game, what is Alfred Pennyworth's main "weapon?"

a. Mop
b. Bucket
c. Tray
d. Feather duster

11 Which human appears in the LEGO Wonder Woman Warrior Battle set?

a. Steve Trevor
b. Clark Kent
c. Lois Lane
d. Alfred Pennyworth

12 What is Alfred's nationality?

a. British
b. Canadian
c. Australian
d. American

13 Which very close friend of Superman is in the LEGO Superman: Black Zero Escape set?

a. Jimmy Olsen
b. Perry White
c. Lois Lane
d. Sam Lane

14 **True or false?** Commissioner Gordon does not know who Batman really is.

I'M READY FOR ACTION!

15 One of Commissioner Gordon's LEGO minifigures holds a Wanted poster—of whom?

a. Lois Lane
b. Alfred
c. The Joker
d. Batman

GENIUS QUESTION

What is the job of Lois Lane's father, Sam Lane?

16 Which of these is Lois Lane?

A.   B.   C.   D.

Answers on page 118

POWERS

What sets Super Heroes apart from ordinary mortals? Their amazing powers! How much do you know about their incredible abilities?

1 Who has the power of super-speed?
a. The Flash
b. Green Arrow
c. Katana
d. Robin

2 Which Super Hero has no superpowers at all?
a. Superman
b. The Flash
c. Wonder Woman
d. Batman

3 Which Super Hero has all these superpowers: X-ray vision, heat vision, flight, super-strength, and super-speed?
a. Aquaman
b. Green Lantern
c. Beast Boy
d. Superman

4 Who was given their powers by an ancient wizard?
a. Superman
b. Shazam!
c. Plastic Man
d. Supergirl

5 True or false? Beast Boy can only transform into either a cat or a dog.

Lex Luthor

6 Which Super Hero can use a power ring to build constructs and fly through space?
a. Hawkman
b. Superboy
c. Firestorm
d. Green Lantern

7 Whose powers were gifts from the Olympian gods?
a. Katana
b. Starfire
c. Wonder Woman
d. Black Canary

8 Which robotic Super Hero is able to access any computer in the world?
a. Blue Beetle b. Cyborg c. Batman d. Nightwing

9 True or false? Black Canary's powerful cry can shatter metal.

10 Match the Super Hero to the power: the ability to stretch and change into any shape.

a. Plastic Man **c.** Zatanna
b. Lightning Lad **d.** Starfire

11 Cosmic Boy's LEGO minifigure uses purple transparent pieces to represent his power—what is it?

a. Heat **c.** Magnetism
b. Cold **d.** Ability to watch 10 TV channels at once

12 True or false? To turn someone into a frog, the magical hero Zatanna simply needs to shout "Frog!"

I MUST BE *THE FASTEST MAN ALIVE!*

13 In the LEGO Lex Luthor Mech Takedown set, which Super Hero uses heat-based powers?

a. Starfire **c.** Batman
b. Firestorm **d.** The Flash

The Flash

14 True or false? Booster Gold uses technology from the future to give himself powers.

15 Which Super Hero gets their powers from special armor made of Nth Metal?

A. **B.** **C.** **D.**

16 Which of these Super Heroes can read minds?

a. Wonder Woman
b. Batman
c. Beast Boy
d. Martian Manhunter

GENIUS QUESTION

What is the Atom's superpower?

Answers on page 118

HIDDEN TALENTS

Even Super Heroes need to relax sometimes. When they are off-duty, they often enjoy some of their lesser-known hobbies and talents.

YOU MIGHT NOT KNOW THE ANSWERS TO THESE... BUT HAVE A GUESS!

1 Which one of these is one of Superman's creative talents?

a. Painting
b. Embroidery
c. Drawing cartoons
d. Pottery

2 Which spicy food is Green Arrow great at cooking?

a. Curry
b. Chili
c. Fajitas
d. Buffalo wings

3 Which Super Hero is such a talented singer that she once toured with a rock band?

a. Black Canary
b. Katana
c. Batgirl
d. Zatanna

4 After a Justice League victory, how does Cyborg like to celebrate?

a. Dancing
b. Singing
c. Holding a pizza-eating contest
d. Playing chess

5 Other than Green Arrow, who is the only Super Hero who can eat Green Arrow's hot food with no trouble?

a. Superman
b. Green Lantern
c. Wonder Woman
d. Batman

6 What is Cyborg's hobby?

a. Stamp collecting
b. Going to the movies
c. Upgrading technology
d. Hiking

7 Which Justice League member's hobby is memorizing trivia?

a. Superman
b. Batman
c. Wonder Woman
d. The Flash

8 **True or false?**

Wonder Woman has a collection of mythical creatures.

13 **True or false?**

Batman is an expert escapologist but Robin is not.

14 Superman builds a highly intelligent robot to play him at which game?

a. Draughts   **c.** Snap

b. Bridge   **d.** Chess

9 What is the name of the dance invented by Batman?

a. The Batusi

b. The Bat Boogie

c. The Bat Trot

d. The Bat Bop

15 What does Shazam! install in the Justice League Watchtower?

a. Table football

b. A pool table

c. A ping-pong table

d. A bowling alley

10 Which flower does Alfred, Batman's butler, have a special talent for growing?

a. Orchids

b. Roses

c. Tulips

d. Dahlias

16 What instrument does Black Canary play?

a. Piano   **c.** Flute

b. Violin   **d.** Harmonica

11 As well as being a master of disguise, what else is the Question an expert in?

a. Poetry   **c.** Acrobatics

b. Piano playing   **d.** Fortune-telling

GENIUS QUESTION

Which sport did Cyborg excel at in high school?

12 Which Super Hero is a keen boxer?

A.   **B.**   **C.**   **D.**

TRUE OR FALSE?
WEAKNESSES

Even the mightiest Super Heroes have their weaknesses. Sometimes the simplest thing can cause them to lose a battle, or stop their powers from working.

1 Superman's main weakness, Kryptonite, is only found in the color green.

2 The Flash's alter ego Barry Allen is always late.

3 Batman is allergic to peanuts.

4 Wonder Woman has no weaknesses.

5 Martian Manhunter's weakness is fire.

6 The Kryptonite piece in the LEGO Kryptonite Interception set is purple and makes Superman laugh.

7 Aquaman is vulnerable to shark attacks.

8 The color red can zap Green Lantern's powers.

9 Zatanna's power can be halted if she is prevented from speaking.

10 Plastic Man loses his powers in extreme heat.

11 Being hungry is The Flash's main weakness.

12 Hawkman is vulnerable to Nth Metal.

13 Kryptonite is not toxic to Supergirl.

14 Raven risks being overpowered by her evil side if she lets her emotions get out of control.

15 The aquatic hero Mera is allergic to fish.

16 Shazam's mighty powers can be stopped by electricity.

17 Firestorm's power to change the shape of objects only works on human-made material.

18 Bizarro's weakness is Blue Kryptonite.

19 Red Hood's main weakness is that he is too nice.

20 Blue Beetle's biggest problem is trying to get his homework done.

21 When Vixen uses her animal powers, her human side can start disappearing.

22 In the LEGO Mighty Micros Superman Vs. Bizarro set, Superman is holding a piece of kryptonite.

23 Cosmic Boy's magnetic power cannot work on wood.

24 There is no limit to the power Star Sapphire's violet ring gives her.

25 Kid Flash risks getting trapped in an energy field called the Speed Force if he goes too fast.

26 The Riddler tries to make The Flash slip up on a banana skin in the LEGO Batman: The Riddler Chase set.

27 Doctor Fate's powers can be stopped by custard-pie attacks.

28 Doctor Fate's powers are reduced if he loses his helmet, the Helmet of Fate.

29 Bat-Mite is very powerful, but his biggest weakness is annoying Batman.

30 Teen Titan Starfire is often confused by Earth customs.

GREEN KRYPTONITE! WHAT DASTARDLY DEED IS THE BOSS PLANNING NEXT?!

Lex Luthor's henchmen

TRAINING

Some Super Heroes are born with their powers, but some have to train hard to gain their amazing skills. Even Superman needs to take time learning how to get the best from his superpowers!

1 In what sort of place did Batman learn his **MARTIAL ARTS SKILLS?**

a. A gym
b. A dojo
c. A school
d. An evening class

2 What was the name of Batman's martial-arts **TEACHER?**

a. Madame Kick
b. Madame Chop
c. Madame Mantis
d. Madame Punch

3 **WHICH VILLAIN** trained alongside Batman in their younger days?

a. Deathstroke
b. Scarecrow
c. Catwoman
d. The Joker

4 Where did **GREEN ARROW** perfect his archery skills?

a. His backyard
b. A desert island
c. Archery class
d. High school

5 True or false? Black Canary trained in hand-to-hand combat in secret.

6 How many other minifigures does the Green Arrow minifigure share his **GREEN BOW AND ARROW WITH?**

a. One
b. Two
c. Three
d. None

7 Who trained Batman in the **ART OF ARCHERY?**

a. Huntress
b. Robin
c. Arsenal
d. Green Arrow

8 Which of these did Batman become expert in as part of **HIS TRAINING?**

a. Forensics
b. Chemistry
c. Disguise
d. All of the above

9 Who trained the already talented acrobat Dick Grayson to be the **CRIME FIGHTER ROBIN?**

a. Batgirl
b. Batman
c. Batwoman
d. Commissioner Gordon

10 True or false? Superman built atomic-powered robots strong enough for him to train with.

11 Which hero was trained as a child to be a warrior by the **IMMORTAL AMAZONS?**

a. Superman **c.** Wonder Woman
b. Hawkman   **d.** Vixen

12 Which **ANCIENT WARRIOR TRADITION** is Katana trained to follow?

a. Samurai
b. Knights of the Round Table
c. Spartan
d. Horsemanship

13 Which powerful hero once lost control of their **TELEPATHIC ABILITIES** during a training exercise?

a. Saturn Girl
b. Martian Manhunter
c. Miss Martian
d. Doctor Fate

14 Which of these costumed heroes did NOT train under top kung fu artist **RICHARD DRAGON?**

a. Huntress   **c.** The Question
b. Batgirl   **d.** Nightwing

15 What did Zatanna's **MAGICIAN FATHER** teach the young Bruce Wayne?

a. Escapology
b. Card tricks
c. How to pull a rabbit from a hat
d. How to make balloon animals

GENIUS QUESTION

When did Alfred Pennyworth receive training in hand-to-hand combat?

Answers on page 119

HERO VEHICLES

For Super Heroes without super-speed, a high-performance vehicle is essential for getting to the bad guys fast. It's just an added bonus if it looks really cool as well!

GENIUS QUESTION

What was Hal Jordan's job before he became Green Lantern?

Green Lantern

1 Who drives the Arrowcar?
a. Arsenal
c. Batman
b. Black Canary
d. Green Arrow

2 In the LEGO Black Manta Deep Sea Strike set, which hero is coming to Aquaman's aid in a customized black submarine?
a. Superman
c. The Flash
b. Wonder Woman
d. Batman

3 What kind of vehicle is Batman's Tumbler?
a. An aircraft
b. A car
c. A boat
d. A submarine

4 What is the vehicle with four caterpillar-tracked feet that Batman uses for rough terrain?
a. CatBat
b. Batplane
c. Knightcrawler
d. Batboat

5 In the LEGO Green Lantern vs. Sinestro set, what sort of vehicle has Green Lantern constructed with his power ring?
a. A Car
b. A Jet
c. A Helicopter
d. A Speedboat

6 In the LEGO Heroes of Justice: Sky-High Battle set, there is a LexCorp helicopter and which other vehicle?
a. Batwing
b. Invisible Jet
c. Batmobile
d. Motorcycle

7 What is the name of the jet in the LEGO Darkseid Invasion set?
a. Invisible Jet
b. Javelin
c. Superjet
d. Batjet

8 What is Black Canary's favorite vehicle?

a. Sports car   c. Jet

b. Motorcycle   d. Speedboat

9 What is the correct name of a LEGO vehicle used by Robin?

a. Redbird Cycle   c. Wonder Whizzer

b. Robin Cycle   d. Chopper

10 Which hero swoops in on a glider to help Batman in the LEGO Batman: Man-Bat Attack set?

a. Robin   b. Batgirl   c. Nightwing   d. Katana

11 Which three-story aircraft does Batman build to transport the entire Justice League?

a. Batplane   b. Batcopter   c. Tri-Plane   d. Flying Fox

12 Which Wonder Woman vehicle is featured in the LEGO Gorilla Grodd Goes Bananas set?

a. Wondermobile   b. Wondercycle   c. Wonderboat   d. Invisible Jet

13 What does Cyborg drive in the LEGO Speed Force Freeze Pursuit set?

a. CyborgCar   b. CyborgCopter   c. CyborgCycle   d. CyborgScooter

14 What color is Superman's vehicle in the LEGO Mighty Micros Superman vs. Bizarro set?

a. Blue   b. Red   c. Black   d. Gold

15 What is the name of Blue Beetle's aircraft, which can also go underwater?

a. Air Beetle   c. The Bug

b. Blueplane   d. Jaime's Amazing Airplane

16 True or false?

This LEGO Batcycle has built-in weapon holders for Batman's gadgets.

Batman

HIDEOUTS

Every self-respecting Super Hero has a special hidden base. Here they can keep costumes and weapons, plus equipment to help them to keep track of bad guys!

CAN I PRESS A BUTTON?

THIS IS THE BAT COMPUTER, NOT THE ROBIN COMPUTER!

1 **Where in Wayne Manor is the entrance to the Batcave?**

a. Under Bruce's bed
b. Behind a grandfather clock
c. Through the cellar
d. Under the living room rug

2 **What is the name of Bruce Wayne's house, situated directly above the Batcave?**

a. Wayne Manor
b. Dunroamin
c. The Bat-House
d. Billionaire Bolthole

3 **The LEGO Batman Classic TV Series Batcave set comes with a Batmobile, Batcycle and which other vehicle?**

a. Batcopter
b. Bat-Tank
c. Batsub
d. Batboat

4 **Atlantis is usually a safe place. But who invades it in the LEGO Battle of Atlantis set?**

a. A blue whale
b. Bizarro
c. A parademon
d. A giant octopus

5 **In the LEGO Batman: Defend the Batcave set, which of these weapons does the Joker NOT use?**

a. Dynamite
b. A robotic penguin
c. Catapult
d. Giant mallet

6 **What is the name of the Justice League's other base, also a museum of their heroic deeds?**

a. Hero Hall
b. Heroland
c. Hall of Justice
d. House of Justice

7 True or false?
There is a dinosaur in the Batcave.

8 Which of these items is a relic of Krypton that Superman keeps in his hideout?
a. Bottled City of Kandor
b. Canned Ham of Lara
c. Sliced Bread of Zod
d. Boxed Throne of Jor-El

9 In the LEGO Batcave: The Penguin and Mr. Freeze's Invasion set, which character has a jet-ski?
a. Robin
b. Batman
c. The Penguin
d. Mr. Freeze

10 What shape is Titans Tower, home to the Teen Titans?
a. A pyramid
b. A star
c. A donut
d. The letter T

11 What does Alfred feed the bats that live in the Batcave?
a. Marshmallows
b. Chicken goujons fried in olive oil
c. Chocolate chip cookies
d. Bananas

12 What did the Legion of Super-Heroes base the design of their future headquarters on?
a. The White House
b. The rocket that carried Superman to Earth
c. The Batmobile
d. A giant LEGO brick

13 What is the name of Superman's secret hideout in the Arctic?
a. Castle of Krypton
b. Supercave
c. Fortress of Solitude
d. Kent Towers

14 Where is the Justice League's Watchtower headquarters located?
a. Themyscira
b. Metropolis
c. Gotham City
d. In Earth's orbit

15 Which mystical hero uses the Tower of Fate?
a. Zatanna
b. Raven
c. Shazam!
d. Doctor Fate

16 Which undersea portion of an American city was Aquaman's base for a while?
a. Sub Diego
b. Blue York
c. Sea Attle
d. Ship Cargo

GENIUS QUESTION
Whose face is seen on a giant playing card in the Batcave?

COSTUMES

Super Heroes wear costumes for many reasons. Their costumes hide their identity, help the public recognize them, and can even scare away bad guys! Could you identify these Super Heroes if you saw them in the street?

1 Who has this symbol on their costume?
a. Robin
b. Superman
c. Batman
d. Aquaman

2 Who has this symbol on their costume?
a. Batman
b. Hawkman
c. Plastic Man
d. Superman

3 Who has this symbol on their costume?
a. Green Arrow
b. Green Lantern
c. Cyborg
d. Beast Boy

4 Who has this symbol on their costume?
a. The Flash
b. Lightning Lad
c. Black Canary
d. Wonder Woman

5 Whose costume usually features a golden tiara with a red star?
a. Batgirl
b. Wonder Woman
c. Supergirl
d. Starfire

6 Which of these heroes does NOT wear an eye mask?
a. Superman
b. Robin
c. Katana
d. Green Arrow

7 Which of these Super Heroes does NOT wear a hood?
a. Wonder Woman
b. Raven
c. Green Arrow
d. Cyborg

GENIUS QUESTION

Besides The Flash, who else has a red costume with a lightning bolt on the chest?

8 Which of these Super Heroes wears a winged helmet?

a. Robin   **b.** Hawkman   **c.** Superman   **d.** Aquaman

9 Whose costume often has a scaly appearance?

a. Aquaman   **c.** Martian Manhunter

b. Beast Boy   **d.** Green Arrow

10 Beast Boy's costume is purple, but which other Teen Titans also wear the color?

a. Cyborg and Robin   **c.** Starfire and Robin

b. Raven and Starfire   **d.** Raven and Cyborg

11 Whose costume features a mask with a red circle, representing the Japanese flag?

a. Mera   **b.** Huntress   **c.** Katana   **d.** Batgirl

12 Which Justice League member's costume features a glowing red eye?

a. Batman   **c.** Cyborg

b. Wonder Woman   **d.** The Flash

13 Which of these Super Heroes has a blue cape?

a. Martian Manhunter   **c.** Batman

b. Superman   **d.** Shazam!

IT'S NOT A COSTUME, IT'S A BATTLE SUIT!

14 True or false? Plastic Man wears sunglasses as part of his costume.

15 Which of these LEGO minifigures does NOT have a costume featuring wings?

a. Hawkman   **c.** Batgirl

b. Blue Beetle   **d.** Space Batman

16 What color cape does Robin often wear?

a. Blue   **c.** Yellow

b. Purple   **d.** Red

Batman

Answers on page 120

BANANA BATTLE

Look out, Gorilla Grodd needs his banana fix! When he starts causing chaos it takes three Super Heroes, plus vehicles and special weapons, to take him down.

1 What is the Invisible Jet armed with?

a. Spring-loaded missiles
b. Lasso of Truth
c. Stud shooters
d. Net

2 True or false?

This LEGO set was the first to feature the famous Invisible Jet.

3 What is the name of Captain Cold's weapon?

a. Cold Master Blaster
b. Fantastic Freeze Gun
c. Ice Is Nice
d. Devastating Ice Shooter

4 How many bananas are included with the set?

a. None
b. Two
c. Seven
d. Four

5 True or false?

Gorilla Grodd is exclusive to this set.

Gorilla Grodd Goes Bananas (76026)

6 The powerful weapon arm of the Bat-Mech has stud shooters and which other weapon?

a. Grappling hook
b. Flick missile
c. Net
d. Batarang

7 Which silhouette is visible on a sticker on the Bat-Mech's readout?

a. Captain Cold
b. The delivery truck
c. Gorilla Grodd
d. A banana

8 True or false?

Batman can launch himself from the Bat-Mech's cockpit.

9 How many LEGO sets does the Bat-Mech feature in?

a. One
b. Two
c. Three
d. Four

10 True or false?

The villains in this set are traditionally enemies of The Flash.

Answers on page 120

HERO TECHNOLOGY

Super Heroes like to stay on the cutting-edge of technology. Having the right high-tech device can be vital in their fight against crime.

1 Green Arrow loves his specialized arrows. Which of these is NOT a real one of his?

a. Boxing glove arrow

b. Glue arrow

c. Cream pie arrow

d. Boomerang arrow

2 In the LEGO Darkseid Invasion set, what is Cyborg armed with?

a. Sword

b. Bow and arrows

c. Batarang

d. Blaster

3 In the LEGO Clash of the Heroes set, what is Batman armed with to take on Superman?

a. Kryptonite blaster

b. Catapult

c. Sharpened carrot

d. Tickling feather

4 **True or false?** The LEGO Batman Classic TV Series Batcave features a lie detector.

5 Barry Allen uses chemicals to compress The Flash's costume and hide it... where?

a. In a ring he wears

b. In his ear

c. Inside his shoe

d. In a pack of gum

6 What does the LEGO Mighty Micros The Flash minifigure use to take on Captain Cold?

a. Banana

b. Grappling hook gun

c. Power Blast energy drink

d. Shark repellent

GENIUS QUESTION

What is the name of the laboratory where Cyborg gained his robotic body?

7 **True or false?**

Cyborg's tech enables him to recover from any wound.

8 What gives Atom's shrinking exosuit its power?

a. Methane gas **b.** Wind turbines **c.** Petroleum **d.** Dwarf stars

9 On his LEGO minifigure, the Atom's incredible exosuit is mainly black, blue, and which other color?

a. Red **b.** Brown **c.** White **d.** Orange

10 In the LEGO Batman: Man-Bat Attack set, Nightwing's glider is equipped with what?

a. A Bat-Signal **c.** Television
b. Two grappling hooks **d.** A juice bar

11 Which of these is a specialized Green Arrow arrow?

a. Grenade arrow **c.** Bazooka arrow
b. Dynamite arrow **d.** Fireworks arrow

12 What does Batman wear for protection in the LEGO Batman: Scarecrow Harvest of Fear set?

a. Armor **c.** Shield
b. Gas mask **d.** Thermal underwear

13 True or false?
Blue Beetle built his armor himself in his garage.

14 Which alien beings created the Blue Beetle scarab technology?

a. The Reach **c.** Kryptonians
b. New Gods **d.** Korugarians

I DON'T NEED ANY FANCY GADGETS. I'M HIGH-TECH ENOUGH MYSELF!

15 What is Cyborg's best known weapon?

a. Cyborangs **c.** A mallet
b. A white noise cannon **d.** A sword

16 In LEGO Batman 3: Beyond Gotham, what transportation device is Cyborg building?

a. Solar-powered bicycle **c.** Jet scooter
b. The "Slideways" teleporter **d.** Time machine

Cyborg

BATCAVE

The Batcave is the ultimate Super Hero hideout. However, even here in his ultra-secure base Batman has to be ready to fight off troublesome super-villains who manage to break in!

1 Which of Batman's vehicles is stored here?

a. Batmobile
b. Batboat
c. Batcopter
d. Batcycle

2 Who is this character?

a. Batgirl
b. Batwoman
c. Huntress
d. Catwoman

3 Which character is the sidecar on the Batcycle designed for?

a. Batman
b. Robin
c. Joker
d. Catwoman

4 True or false?

This is the only LEGO Batmobile to have a red bat-symbol.

Batman™ Classic TV Series—Batcave (76052)

5 Who are the portraits beside the bookcase of?

a. Bruce Wayne and Selina Kyle
b. Thomas and Martha Wayne
c. Clark Kent and Lois Lane
d. Dick Grayson and Barbara Gordon

6 Alfred is on the Batphone, which is a direct line to...?

a. Batgirl
b. Superman
c. Commissioner Gordon
d. The Joker

7 What is concealed under this bust of William Shakespeare?

a. The button that opens the Batcave entrance
b. A note of Batman's secret identity
c. Bruce Wayne's credit cards
d. Alfred's duster

8 True or false?

A colony of real bats lives in the Batcave.

9 True or false?

As well as Batman, this set contains a Bruce Wayne minifigure.

10 What is the Joker's favorite poisonous potion?

a. Joker Tea
b. Joker Soup
c. Joker Serum
d. Joker Venom

TRUE OR FALSE?
ORIGIN STORIES

Behind every Super Hero or super-villain is a fascinating story! Can you tell the facts from the fiction?

1 Baby Superman is rocketed to Earth from the Planet Apokolips.

2 The infant Superman crash-lands in Missouri when he arrives on Earth.

3 Batman comes from outer space.

4 Martha Kent makes Clark's glasses from recycled parts of his rocket.

5 Bruce Wayne adopts the persona of a bat because it is his favorite animal.

6 Bruce Wayne decides to fight crime after one of his boats is stolen.

7 Harvey Dent is a lawyer before he becomes the villain Two-Face.

8 Cyborg has always been a robot.

9 Barry Allen becomes The Flash during a lightning strike, while he is working in his lab.

10 Wonder Woman gets her powers after being exposed to radiation.

11 The Joker is a children's entertainer before he becomes Batman's archenemy.

12 Harley Quinn is the Joker's psychiatrist before she joins him in his life of crime.

13 Bruce Wayne adopts young Dick Grayson.

14 Aquaman's mother was the Queen of Atlantis.

15 Arthur Curry, alias Aquaman, grows up in Atlantis.

16 Poison Ivy has always been immune to poisons and toxins.

17 Lightning Lad, Saturn Girl, and Cosmic Boy form the Legion of Super-Heroes.

18 Billy Batson is turned into the hero Shazam! by a wizard.

19 Plastic Man gets his amazing elastic powers by falling into a vat of chemicals.

20 Barbara Gordon becomes Batgirl because her father doesn't want her to join the police.

21 The villain Sinestro starts out as a hero.

22 Katana learns her martial arts skills after deciding to become a hero.

23 Jaime Reyes becomes Blue Beetle when a mysterious scarab beetle attaches itself to his body.

24 Black Manta trains himself to breathe underwater.

25 Beast Boy's Super Hero abilities are a side effect of the treatment he receives for a rare illness.

26 Bane grows up in prison.

27 Oliver Queen uses his family business to make special trick arrows as the hero Green Arrow.

28 Hal Jordan's power ring selects him to be Green Lantern.

29 The Penguin grows up in a zoo.

30 Jason Todd becomes Red Hood because he is a fan of Robin Hood.

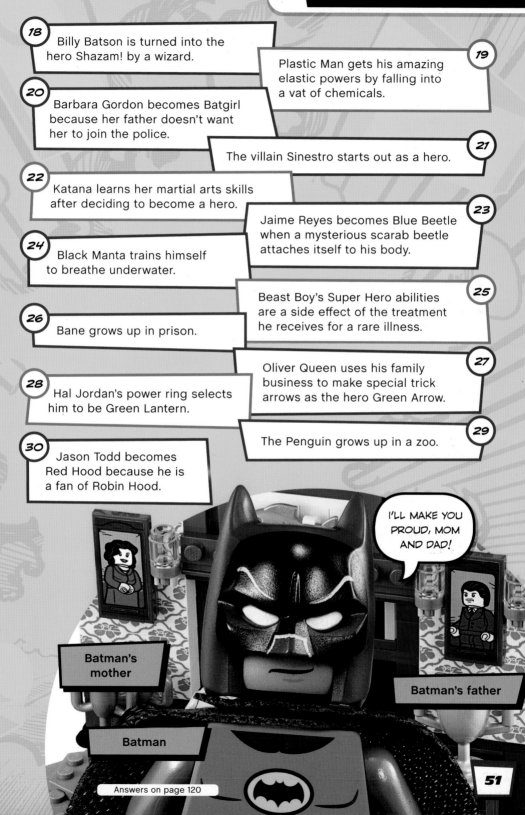

I'LL MAKE YOU PROUD, MOM AND DAD!

Batman's mother

Batman's father

Batman

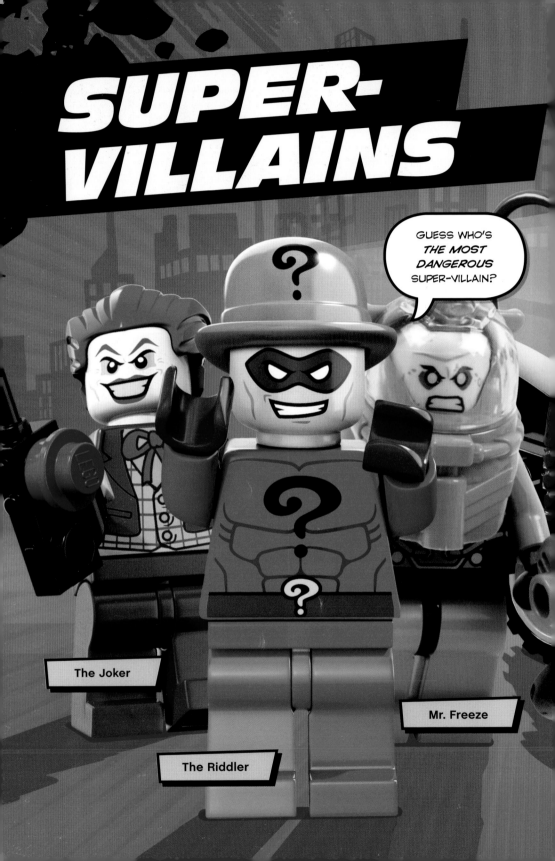

CRAZY CROOKS

This parade of wacky super-villains are always giving Super Heroes headaches by committing crazy crimes and causing general chaos!

1 In the LEGO® Dynamic Duo: Funhouse Escape set, Harley Quinn's costume is mainly in **WHICH COLORS?**

a. Pink and white

b. Black and white

c. Black and red

d. Purple and orange

2 What is **TWO-FACE** stealing in the LEGO Batmobile and the Two-Face Chase set?

a. A safe

b. Batman's Utility Belt

c. A treasure chest

d. The Flash's lunch

3 What is Scarecrow's **FAVORITE WEAPON?**

a. Fear gas

b. Joy buzzer

c. Harpoon

d. Mallet

4 Which villain has a **BRIGHTLY COLORED** motorbike in the LEGO Gotham City Cycle Chase?

a. The Joker

b. Harley Quinn

c. The Penguin

d. Scarecrow

5 Who is **HARLEY QUINN** facing in her LEGO Mighty Micros battle?

a. Batman

b. Alfred

c. Robin

d. The Joker

6 What symbol does the Riddler display all over his **GREEN COSTUME?**

a. Exclamation marks

b. Stars

c. Bats

d. Question marks

7 What sort of aircraft does **SCARECROW** have in the LEGO The Batcopter: The Chase for Scarecrow set?

a. Helicopter

b. Hot air balloon

c. Zeppelin

d. Biplane

8 Who is **SCARECROW'S** alter ego?

a. Victor Fries

b. Edward Nigma

c. Jonathan Crane

d. Axel Walker

9 True or false? One of Harley Quinn's LEGO minifigures is wearing roller skates.

10 WHICH VILLAIN
joins the Joker and Harley Quinn in the LEGO: Dynamic Duo Funhouse Escape set?

a. Bane
b. The Riddler
c. Clayface
d. Trickster

11 Who is POISON IVY'S BEST FRIEND?

a. Harley Quinn
b. Cheetah
c. Talia al Ghūl
d. Giganta

12 If Poison Ivy achieved her ultimate goal, what would COVER THE PLANET?

a. Water
b. Shopping malls
c. Plants
d. Donut shops

13 How does Two-Face make IMPORTANT DECISIONS?

a. Asks his henchmen
b. Flips a coin
c. Draws lots
d. Asks the Joker

14 What is the Trickster's GREATEST INVENTION?

a. Whoopee cushions
b. Clockwork teeth
c. Anti-gravity boots
d. Rapid-fire catapults

15 What is Scarecrow ARMED WITH in the LEGO Batman: Scarecrow Harvest of Fear set?

a. Dynamite
b. Batarang
c. Sword
d. Pitchfork

16 What is the COSTUMED IDENTITY of Jervis Tetch?

a. The Mad Hatter
b. The Riddler
c. Clayface
d. The Trickster

GENIUS QUESTION
Who is the alter ego of Two-Face?

WHAT'S FAST BUT SLOWS YOU RIGHT DOWN? QUICKSAND!

The Riddler

55

ARKHAM ASYLUM

The world's craziest criminals are kept behind bars in Arkham Asylum. Unfortunately, they occasionally escape!

1 What is the name of the symbol that summons Batman to the scene of a crime?

a. Bat-Alarm
b. Bat-Lamp
c. Bat-O-Gram
d. Bat-Signal

4 True or false?

There have been more than 50 LEGO Batman minifigures.

2 What is Harley Quinn's real name?

a. Harriet Quirk
b. Helen Quick
c. Harleen Quinzel
d. Hortense Quadrille

5 How many sets have the Joker and Batman appeared in together?

a. Eight
b. Ten
c. Twelve
d. Fourteen

3 True or false?

This security van is specially equipped to hold the Joker.

Batman™: Arkham Asylum Breakout (10937)

6 What is the Penguin wearing on his face?

a. False mustache
b. Monocle
c. Scuba mask
d. Swimming goggles

7 True or false?

Poison Ivy has featured in every Arkham Asylum LEGO set.

8 What is unusual about Scarecrow's original LEGO minifigure?

a. It has a pumpkin head
b. It cannot be taken apart
c. It has purple hair
d. It has a glow-in-the-dark head

ARKHAM ASYLUM

9 Who was Arkham Asylum named after?

a. Elizabeth Arkham, the founder's mother
b. Maude Arkham, the founder's sister
c. Noah Arkham, the founder's boatbuilder
d. Bob Arkham, the founder's gardener

10 True or false?

This weapon is called a bo staff.

57

ALIEN TERRORS

Earth is always under threat from power-crazy evil aliens longing to conquer the planet and add it to their galactic empires!

1

Which corrupt Kryptonian leads a team of villains to Earth to fight Superman?

a. Captain Cod
b. Private Pod
c. Lieutenant Log
d. General Zod

RESISTANCE IS USELESS, FEEBLE EARTHLINGS. I AM INVINCIBLE!

2

What has Sinestro stolen in the LEGO Green Lantern vs. Sinestro set?

a. A power ring
b. Green Lantern's battery
c. A Mother Box
d. The Batmobile

3

What color light does Sinestro control with his power ring?

a. Yellow   b. Green   c. Red   d. Violet

4

And which emotion fuels Sinestro's light powers?

a. Willpower   b. Fear   c. Hope   d. Rage

5

What color are Darkseid's eyes in his LEGO bigfig?

a. Blue   b. White   c. Purple   d. Red

6

What sort of troops does Darkseid usually send to do his dirty work?

a. Red Lanterns   c. Parademons
b. Clones   d. Evil robots

Darkseid

7

Which Space Hog bike-riding bad guy is in the LEGO Superman & Krypto Team-Up set?

a. Black Manta   c. Lobo
b. Lex Luthor   d. Doomsday

8 True or false?

No one is immune to Darkseid's powerful Omega Beams, fired from his eyes.

9 Which animal is pretty much the only thing that space assassin Lobo really loves?

a. Space scorpion   **c.** Space horse

b. Space dolphin   **d.** Space cockroach

10 Which hero is Doomsday taking on in his LEGO Mighty Micros battle?

a. Batman   **c.** Wonder Woman

b. Robin   **d.** Batgirl

11 Which hero is the main enemy of the alien villain Doomsday?

a. Batman   **c.** The Flash

b. Superman   **d.** Green Lantern

Sinestro

12 What is the name of Darkseid's Apokoliptian right-hand man and enforcer?

a. Desaad   **c.** Bleez

b. Granny Goodness   **d.** Lightseid

13 Ferocious alien Arkillo is a member of which team?

a. Red Lanterns   **c.** Star Sapphires

b. Orange Lanterns   **d.** Sinestro Corps

GENIUS QUESTION

Which villainous alien is Darkseid's uncle?

14 Who is leading the alien attack in the LEGO Flying Fox: Batmobile Airlift Attack set?

a. Steppenwolf   **c.** Brainiac

b. Darkseid   **d.** Doomsday

15 What emotion powers Larfleeze, the Orange Lantern?

a. Anger   **b.** Fear   **c.** Greed   **d.** Envy

16 Which bad guy is the leader of the Red Lanterns?

a. Atrocitus   **b.** Sinestro   **c.** Lobo   **d.** Doomsday

59

THE WEIRD AND THE DEADLY

Villains come in all shapes and sizes. Some are dangerous mercenaries, some are scary monsters, and some are just plain weird!

1 Who is the God of War, featuring in the LEGO Wonder Woman Warrior Battle set?

a. Zeus b. Hermes c. Ares d. Steve Trevor

2 Which villain is trying to evade justice in the LEGO Batboat Harbor Pursuit set?

a. Deathstroke c. Clayface
b. Harley Quinn d. The Penguin

3 Which villain dresses like a caveman and has been carrying out evil schemes since prehistoric times?

a. Vandal Savage c. Crazy Quilt
b. Solomon Grundy d. Black Manta

4 Lady Shiva is expert at what?

a. Car mechanics c. Stamp collecting
b. Martial arts d. Flower arranging

5 Which shape-changing villainous alter ego has Basil Karlo adopted?

a. Deathstroke c. Black Mask
b. Solomon Grundy d. Clayface

6 Who is lethal marksman Deadshot's alter ego?

a. Lloyd Fawton
b. Floyd Lawton
c. Walt Floydon
d. Waldo Flyton

GENIUS QUESTION
Which very unjust team has included Wizard, Solomon Grundy, and Gentleman Ghost?

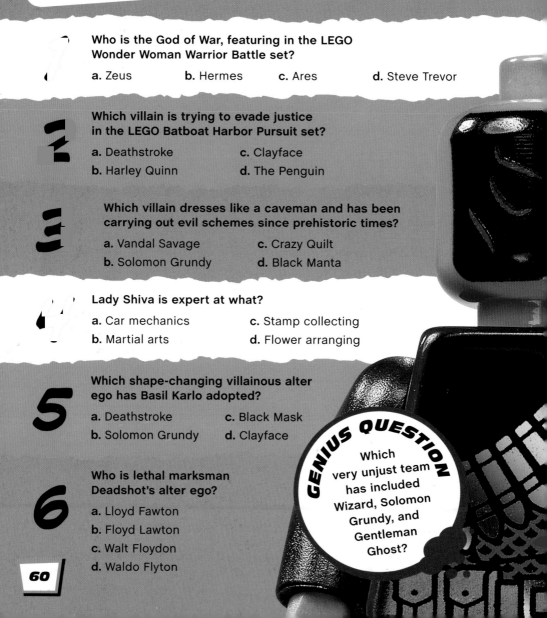

7 What is the correct spelling of the name of the mischievous imp who comes to our dimension to pester Superman?

a. Mr. Mixypetal

b. Mr. Lipymix

c. Mr. Mxyzptlk

d. Mr. Kltpzyxm

8 What kind of spooky creature is Solomon Grundy?

a. Zombie

b. Vampire

c. Werewolf

d. Leprechaun

9 Solomon Grundy takes his name from a nursery rhyme character, born on which day?

a. Monday

b. Tuesday

c. Saturday

d. Thursday

10 Roman Sionis is the real name of a villain called Black Mask. What is Black Mask's occupation?

a. Car thief

b. Doctor

c. Magician

d. Gang Boss

11 Which spooky former highwayman appears in the LEGO Harley Quinn Cannonball Attack set?

a. Solomon Grundy

b. Black Hand

c. Gentleman Ghost

d. Crazy Quilt

12 Who is notorious for being the world's deadliest mercenary?

a. Deadloss

b. Deathstroke

c. Deathdealer

d. Deadwrong

13 What is Deadshot armed with in the LEGO Gotham City Cycle Chase set?

a. Batarang

b. Rocket launcher

c. Boomerang

d. Magic wand

14 Who is said to be the best martial artist in the world?

a. Solomon Grundy

b. Captain Cold

c. Lady Shiva

d. Alfred

15 True or false?

The bigger the villainess Giganta grows, the cleverer she becomes.

Deadshot

16 True or false?

Wilson Slade is Deadshot's real name.

Answers on page 121

TRUE OR FALSE?
ARCHENEMIES

Every Super Hero has a super-villain who is obsessed with defeating them. And even though they fail time after time, these bad guys never seem to know when to give up!

1 Cheetah is Wonder Woman's archenemy.

2 Superman's archenemy is Darkseid.

3 Batman does not have an archenemy.

4 In the LEGO Bane Toxic Truck Attack set, Bane is a minifigure.

5 Aquaman's archenemy is the masked Black Manta.

6 The Flash has an evil opposite.

7 Batgirl's most frequent foe is Killer Moth.

8 Green Arrow's archenemy is Arsenal.

9 Deathstroke is Nightwing's main foe.

10 Calculator declared himself the archenemy of Barbara Gordon while she was Oracle.

11 Starfire's main enemy is her brother.

12 Green Lantern's bitter enemy Sinestro used to be a Green Lantern.

13 Black Adam's powers are the same as those of his archenemy, Shazam!

14 The Justice League's foremost enemy is Darkseid.

15 Batman's archenemy appears in the LEGO Dynamic Duo Funhouse Escape set.

16 The LEGO Speed Force Freeze Pursuit set contains The Flash's nemesis Reverse-Flash.

17 Beast Boy's main foe is Raven.

18 Supergirl frequently battles Superman.

19 Back on Krypton, General Zod was the archenemy of Superman's father Jor-El.

20 One of Hawkman and Hawkgirl's most persistent foes is Mr. Ghost, Esquire.

21 Rather than have one main foe, Huntress is the enemy of all gangsters.

ONE DAY I'LL DEFEAT AQUAMAN ONCE AND FOR ALL!

22 Aquaman's archenemy, Black Manta, can fire energy blasts.

23 Captain Cold sees The Flash as his archfoe, even if the speedster doesn't feel the same way!

24 Firestorm's main enemy is Mr. Freeze.

25 The New God Orion's greatest threat is his uncle, Highfather.

26 Although both are on the wrong side of the law, Catwoman and Black Mask are bitter enemies.

27 Black Canary's archenemy is another bird-themed character, the Penguin.

28 Bane has been the main enemy of all the different Robins.

29 Batman fights the Joker in the LEGO Batwing Battle over Gotham City set.

Black Manta

30 Lex Luthor is strong enough to take on Superman.

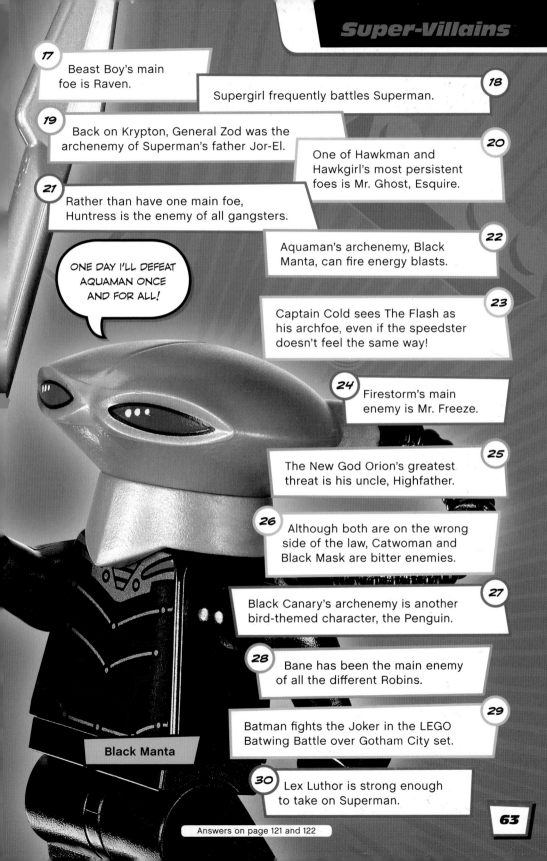

63

VILLAINS' LAIRS

Every criminal needs a hideout—a special place where they can plan their next crime and then run off to, hoping to avoid being captured by a Super Hero!

1 True or false?
The Joker's base is called the Jokercave.

2 What is the name of the
PENGUIN'S NOTORIOUS LAIR?

a. Antarctic Falls
b. Flipper Factory
c. Iceberg Lounge
d. Cobblepot Towers

3 And what is the
PENGUIN'S BASE?

a. A nightclub
b. A luxury yacht
c. A mountain fortress
d. A zoo enclosure

4 True or false?
Penguin's lair features a pool for his pet seals and penguins.

GENIUS QUESTION
Where is the alien super-villain Sinestro's home base?

5 What sort of
BOOBY TRAP
does the desert hideout in LEGO Rescue from Rā's al Ghūl set have?

a. Trapdoor
b. Swinging ax
c. Net
d. Giant boxing glove

6 What shape is
BIZARRO WORLD,
home to Superman's clone?

a. Sphere
b. Cylinder
c. Cube
d. Pyramid

7 What happens to the
JUSTICE LEAGUE
(apart from Superman) on Bizarro World?

a. They lose their powers
b. They are made even stronger
c. They become invisible
d. They fall asleep

8 Lex Luthor does most of his plotting at
LEXCORP TOWER.
How tall is it?

a. 50 stories
b. 75 stories
c. 80 stories
d. 96 stories

9 What is the drawback of the Legion of Doom's **HALL OF DOOM?**

a. No cafeteria

b. Not enough parking spaces

c. Too easy for heroes to get in

d. Next door to a police station

10 How many tentacles does **BRAINIAC'S SKULL SHIP** have?

a. Two   b. Four   c. Six   d. Eight

11 General Zod's base, **THE BLACK ZERO,** was a former prison ship from where?

a. Apokolips

b. New Genesis

c. Korugar

d. The Phantom Zone

12 On which continent is **GORILLA CITY,** hometown of Gorilla Grodd?

a. Asia

b. Europe

c. Africa

d. North America

13 Where does Darkseid **CALL HOME?**

a. Qward

b. Apokolips

c. New Genesis

d. Krypton

14 In which unpleasant part of **GOTHAM CITY** does Killer Croc make his lair?

a. Wayne Manor

b. Crime Alley

c. The sewers

d. Gotham City Police Department

15 It's not an official lair, but many criminal plots are hatched in **ARKHAM ASYLUM.** Where is the asylum based?

a. Gotham City

b. Metropolis

c. Keystone City

d. Central City

16 In the LEGO The Bat-Tank: Riddler and Bane's hideout, what does the **SIGN** on the gate say?

a. Welcome!

b. Stay out!

c. No bats allowed

d. Pass pizzas through gate

The Joker's Funhouse

WATCH OUT!

DANG AH!

LEX LUTHOR

Superman's archenemy is not a mighty alien warlord, but a "mere" Earthling. Lex Luthor is determined to become the planet's most powerful being—and that means defeating the Man of Steel!

AT LAST! WITH MY WAR SUIT AND DECONSTRUCTOR GUN, I'M A MATCH FOR THE PESKY MAN OF STEEL!

Lex Luthor

1 Who has Lex Luthor captured in the LEGO Superman vs. Power Armor Lex set?

a. Lois Lane
b. Batman
c. Wonder Woman
d. The Flash

2 Official LexCorp vehicles usually come in which colors?

a. Black and white
b. Red and blue
c. Black and green
d. Black and blue

3 Lex Luthor's LEGO minifigures often show him as bald, but when he has hair, what color is it?

a. Black
b. Brown
c. Yellow
d. Orange

4 Which city is the home of Lex Luthor's company LexCorp?

a. Gotham City
b. Central City
c. Coast City
d. Metropolis

5 True or false?
Lex Luthor uses the money from his tech corporation to invent ways to defeat Superman.

6 Lex Luthor, tired of being defeated by the Justice League, starts which evil team?

a. No More Heroes
b. The Legion of Doom
c. Justice for Villains
d. Bad Squad

7 True or false?
Lex Luthor has been President of the United States.

8 Which two villains were the first to join Luthor's team?

a. Joker and Harley Quinn
b. Darkseid and Doomsday
c. Black Manta and Sinestro
d. Cheetah and Trickster

9 In the LEGO Batman & Superman vs. Lex Luthor set, what are the main colors of Lex's robotic vehicle?

a. Pink and blue
b. Purple and green
c. Orange and red
d. Blue and white

10 Which villain performs so well at team tryouts that Lex becomes jealous and decides not to take him on?

a. Captain Cold
b. Deathstroke
c. The Joker
d. The Penguin

11 Which alien hero falls under Lex's control before rejecting him?

a. Supergirl
b. Starfire
c. Miss Martian
d. Martian Manhunter

12 Who does Luthor team up with in order to steal Kryptonite from the Batcave?

a. The Penguin   c. The Joker
b. Mr. Freeze   d. Harley Quinn

13 What is said (possibly by himself!) to be Lex Luthor's greatest power?

a. His mind
b. His dress sense
c. His money
d. His physical strength

14 In the LEGO Heroes of Justice: Sky High Battle set, Lex flies in which LexCorp-branded vehicle?

a. Helicopter   c. Private jet
b. Blimp   d. Spaceship

15 What is Lex Luthor's war suit lined with?

a. Lead
b. Steel
c. Green Kryptonite
d. Blue Kryptonite

16 True or false?

Lex Luthor is on a mission to destroy humanity.

GENIUS QUESTION

Lex Luthor's sister and daughter have the same name—what is it?

EVIL GADGETS AND TECHNOLOGY

Instead of trying to make the world a better place, these no-good geniuses create weapons and technology to help them commit crimes or gain power!

How is LEX THOR hoping to take down Superman in the LEGO Superman Vs. Power Armor Lex set?

a. Laser cannon

b. Kryptonite gun

c. Giant mallet hands

d. A strongly worded speech

Why did Captain Cold invent his COLD GUN?

a. To make his own popsicles

b. To slow down The Flash

c. To beat his frenemy Heat Wave

d. To cool down hot soup

What weapon does Lex Luthor use to destroy BLACK, SHINY OBJECTS?

a. Deconstructor

b. Smasher

c. Deshinynator

d. Lexinator

4 Which of these does the Joker's LEGO Ultrabuild figure's **BLASTER** NOT fire?

a. Laughing gas

c. Smoke bombs

b. Venom

d. Batarangs

5 Which of these **BOOBY TRAPS** does NOT feature in the LEGO Dynamic Duo Funhouse Escape set?

a. Trapdoor

c. Giant boxing glove

b. Swinging hammer

d. Moving floor

6 What traps **AQUAMAN** in the LEGO Arctic Batman vs. Mr. Freeze set?

a. Fish tank

c. Trapdoor

b. Ice prison

d. Cage

7 Which of these is NOT one of Captain Boomerang's custom **WEAPONIZED BOOMERANGS?**

a. Rocket boomerang

d. Cream pie boomerang

b. Lightning boomerang

c. Explosive boomerang

8 In the LEGO Batman: The Penguin Face Off set, what is the Penguin holding, apart from an **UMBRELLA?**

a. Fishing net

c. Shrink ray

b. Freeze gun

d. Detonator

9 What is the name of

BLACK MANTA'S

undersea transport in the LEGO Black Manta Deep Sea Strike set?

a. Sea Saucer

c. Mantamobile

b. Sea Cup

d. Black Sub

10 In the LEGO Darkseid Invasion set, what is Darkseid's

HOVER DESTROYER
armed with ?

a. Laser shooters

b. Kryptonite gun

c. Cannonball shooter

d. Laughing gas bombs

11 # BRAINIAC
is as clever as his name suggests, but what technology is he most famous for?

a. Enlarging

c. Time travel

b. Shrinking

d. Weapons

12 What does Scarecrow build to **TRAP THE FARMER** in the LEGO Batman: Scarecrow Harvest of Fear set?

a. Fear gas tank

c. Sticky trap

b. Metal cage

d. Super-strong net

13 Killer Moth builds an array of

GADGETS,
inspired by Batman. Which of these does he create?

a. Moth-Signal

b. Mothmobile

c. Moth-Cave

d. All of the above

14 The "mild-mannered" Ventriloquist uses his **DUMMY** to do all his dirty work—what is its name?

a. Arnold

c. Goodfella

b. Scarface

d. Corleone

15 Which wacky gadget does **TRICKSTER** NOT use to fight the Justice League?

a. Giant chattering teeth

b. Stink bomb

c. Laughing gas missile

d. Anti-gravity shoes

16 True or false? Superman-gone-wrong clone Bizarro was created by a LexCorp weapon.

Robot penguin

GENIUS QUESTION
Which villain has invented a "cocoon gun" that fires sticky webs?

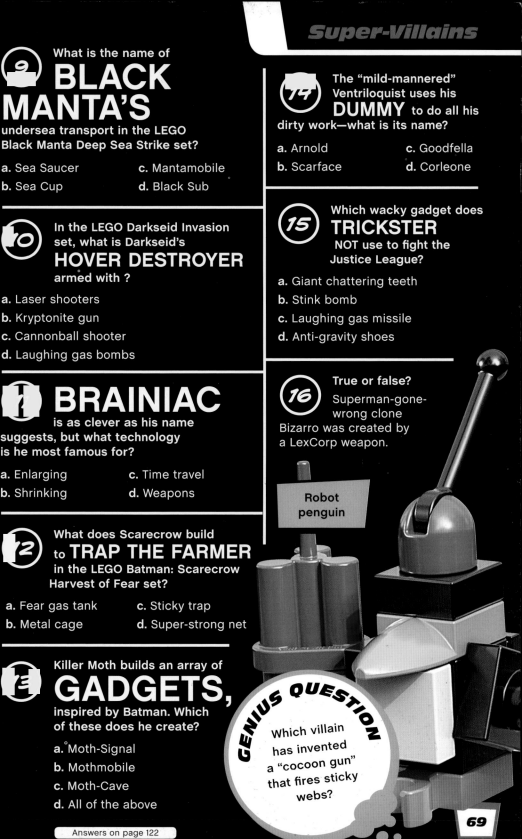

69

Answers on page 122

TRUE OR FALSE?
EPIC BATTLES

There comes a point in every super-villain's career when they have to face a Super Hero in battle. But have they got what it takes to come out victorious?

1 In the LEGO Superman: Battle of Smallville set, Superman is facing two evil Kryptonians.

3 Batman has prepared to fight Wonder Woman in the LEGO Clash of the Heroes set.

2 In the LEGO Batman: Man-Bat Attack set, Batman confronts the villain in the Batmobile.

5 In the LEGO Darkseid Invasion set, no less than four heroes are facing the mighty Darkseid.

4 In the LEGO Green Lantern vs. Sinestro set, Sinestro is ready for battle with a weapon construct.

7 There are no humans battling in the LEGO Brainiac Attack set.

6 When the Justice League are sent to a black hole by Sinestro, The Flash has to battle him alone.

9 The Flash's LEGO Mighty Micros battle is against the Reverse-Flash.

8 In Batman's two LEGO Mighty Micros sets, he faces Catwoman and Bane.

11 Killer Moth's LEGO Mighty Micros vehicle is armed with a sting.

10 In his LEGO Mighty Micros battle, Superman faces his strange, imperfect clone, Bizarro.

13 In the LEGO Batman: The Penguin Face Off set, Batman is armed with a harpoon.

12 Lex Luthor formed the Legion of Doom because he was sick of losing battles to Super Heroes.

15 The Bizarro League teams up with Darkseid's forces against its Justice League counterparts.

14 Cyborg once defeated Darkseid by using his own Omega Beams against him.

17 Superman's opponent in the LEGO Superman Metropolis Showdown set is Lex Luthor.

16 Batman's first battle with the Justice League is against a team of villains assembled by the mischievous Bat-Mite.

18 The Justice League defeats the Legion of Doom in its first battle.

19 The Legion of Doom escapes the battlefield on Gorilla Grodd's hover platform.

20 When the inmates at Arkham Asylum riot, security guard Aaron Cash is ready for battle with a handy weapon!

21 In the LEGO Battle of Atlantis set, the Atlantean Guards are armed with spears.

22 In the LEGO Flying Fox: Batmobile Airlift Attack set, Steppenwolf is sending Parademons to battle the Justice League.

23 Superman is ready for aerial battle with Killer Moth in the LEGO Batman: Scarecrow Harvest of Fear set.

24 Batman battled Superman when the Man of Steel was being controlled by Brainiac.

25 On another occasion, Batman saved Superman from Brainiac's control by electrocuting the villain.

Superman

26 The Justice League once battled a giant robot Joker.

27 On one occasion, Brainiac beats the Justice League in battle and shrinks Earth.

28 Steppenwolf is the bad guy in the LEGO Heroes of Justice: Sky High Battle set.

29 Lex Luthor once helped Brainiac to combine all the different color Lantern powers to make a shrink ray.

Brainiac

30 In the LEGO Wonder Woman Warrior Battle set, Wonder Woman and Ares are armed with swords and shields.

INFAMOUS HEISTS

Crafty crooks like the Penguin spend most of their time plotting their next crime. Of course, some masterplans are more successful than others!

1 Which member of Arkham Asylum staff helps the **VILLAINS ESCAPE** in the LEGO Batman: Arkham Asylum Breakout set?

a. Dr. Jonathan Crane
b. Dr. Hugo Strange
c. Jeremiah Arkham
d. Dr. Harleen Quinzel

2 **THE PENGUIN** steals a diamond in the LEGO Batman: The Penguin Face Off set. What shape is his boat?

a. Duck
b. Swan
c. Eagle
d. Penguin

MY COLD GUN WILL GIVE YOU THE CHILLS!

Mr. Freeze

3 The Penguin fakes his own death in order to rob his own **MEMORIAL FUND**. What was the fund supposed to be in aid of?

a. Retired criminals
b. Injured Super Heroes
c. Endangered birds
d. War veterans

4 In one of the Penguin's **EARLIEST CRIMES,** how did he smuggle two priceless paintings out of a museum?

a. In his umbrella's handle
b. Under his top hat
c. By carrier pigeon
d. Inside a newspaper

5 What has **DEATHSTROKE STOLEN** in the LEGO Batboat Harbor Pursuit set?

a. Swords
b. Diamonds
c. Money
d. Robin

6 When the Joker comes up with the idea of charging **FELLOW CRIMINALS** to carry out his crimes, what does he call the group?

a. Crime Collective
b. Gotham Gangsters Unite
c. Joker's Dozen
d. Crime-of-the-Month Club

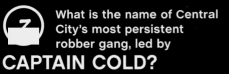 **7** What is the name of Central City's most persistent robber gang, led by

CAPTAIN COLD?

a. The Freeze-Outs **c.** The Felons

b. The Rogues **d.** The Burglarizers

8 Captain Cold competes with which other villain to carry out the

BIGGEST CRIME SPREE

to impress a local TV star?

a. Mirror Master **c.** Trickster

b. Weather Wizard **d.** Heat Wave

9 The Riddler once "kidnapped" four "babies" in order to score himself a

GIANT RANSOM.

What were they?

a. Egyptian idols **c.** Antique violins

b. Precious stones **d.** Pedigree puppies

10 The Riddler once tried to search for hidden gangster treasure under Gotham City.

What was his **COVER STORY?**

a. Presenting a basement-based TV prank show

b. Posed as a sewer engineer

c. Studying urban archaeology

d. Hunting Killer Croc

11 Which creatures does the Joker alter with

CHEMICALS

to look like him, hoping to score a fortune by selling the patent?

a. Cows **c.** Dogs

b. Fish **d.** Bats

 12 In the LEGO Batman and the Two-Face Chase set, which building has Two-Face broken a

SAFE OUT OF?

a. Gotham City Police Department

b. The Batcave

c. Arkham Asylum

d. A bank

 13 Who did

SCARECROW

team up with to rob a bank, before sneaking onto the Justice League's Watchtower satellite?

a. Harley Quinn **c.** The Riddler

b. Poison Ivy **d.** Mirror Master

 14 True or false?

The Bat-Signal was once stolen from Gotham City Police Department Headquarters.

 15 What is Catwoman's

FAVORITE THING TO STEAL?

a. Emeralds **c.** Priceless art

b. Gold bullion **d.** Diamonds

 16 Catwoman once tried to loot Wayne Manor after winning Alfred's heart while

DISGUISED AS A...

a. Nurse **c.** Cat

b. Maid **d.** Movie star

 **17** Which thief's weapon of choice when carrying out heists is a

TRICK UMBRELLA?

a. The Penguin **c.** The Riddler

b. Harley Quinn **d.** Scarecrow

73

KINGS OF THE UNDERWORLD

There are those who make crime their business—unscrupulous villains who rule their underworld empires with iron fists.

GENIUS QUESTION

What gives Bane his superhuman strength?

1 In the LEGO The Bat-Tank: The Riddler and Bane's Hideout set, what vehicle is Bane riding?

a. Motorcycle **b.** Bicycle **c.** Scooter **d.** Jet ski

2 What has Mr. Freeze stolen in the LEGO Batman's Buggy: The Escape of Mr. Freeze set?

a. Bananas **c.** Money

b. Diamonds **d.** A Batsuit

3 True or false? Marks on the Penguin's sub in the LEGO Robin's Scuba Jet: Attack of the Penguin set show how many times he has defeated Batman.

4 What has the Penguin got with him in the LEGO Batman: Arkham Asylum Breakout set?

a. A fish and an umbrella **c.** A fish and a harpoon

b. An umbrella and a banana **d.** An umbrella and dynamite

I PLAN TO BE A VILLAIN FOREVER!

5 What is the most iconic part of Bane's costume?

a. Belt **b.** Boots **c.** Cape **d.** Mask

6 What is Mr. Freeze's weapon in the LEGO Arctic Batman vs. Mr. Freeze: Aquaman on Ice set?

a. Harpoon **c.** Freeze gun

b. Mallet **d.** Popsicle cannon

Rā's al Ghūl

7 Which of these villains is a member of Captain Cold's Rogues gang?

a. Killer Frost **c.** Firefly

b. Mr. Freeze **d.** Heat Wave

I'M LOOKING TO BREAK THE BAT!

8 True or false?

The Penguin wears glasses.

9 Who is Rā's al Ghūl's partner in crime in the LEGO Batman: Rescue from Rā's al Ghūl set?

a. Captain Cold   c. Mr. Freeze

b. The Penguin   d. Talia al Ghūl

10 What is Rā's al Ghūl's weapon in the LEGO Batman: Rescue From Rā's al Ghūl set?

a. Blaster   c. Sword

b. Custard pie   d. Bow and arrows

11 True or false?

The Penguin is a master of martial arts.

Bane

12 What is Rā's al Ghūl's nickname?

a. The Demon's Head   c. The Ghulster

b. Al   d. Living Legend

13 What is the alter ego of the Penguin?

a. Victor Fries   c. Leonard Snart

b. Oswald Cobblepot   d. Mick Rory

14 What color is Bane's Tumbler in the LEGO The Bat vs. Bane: Tumbler Chase set?

a. Black   b. Tan   c. Gray   d. Blue

15 In Captain Cold's LEGO Mighty Micros battle with The Flash, he has his Cold Gun and what else?

a. Ice cream   c. Money

b. Banana   d. Energy drink

16 What do the Condiment King's guns fire?

a. Mayo and soy sauce   c. Sweet chilli sauce and BBQ sauce

b. Ketchup and mustard   d. Salt and pepper

75

TRUE OR FALSE?
THE JOKER

Batman's archfoe has a permanent smile on his face, but Batman does not find the Joker at all funny. This villain's crimes leave Gotham City littered with grinning victims, joy buzzers, and custard pies!

1 The Joker's alter ego is Billy Gigglesworth.

2 Harley Quinn falls for the Joker in Arkham Asylum.

3 The Joker has two large pictures of himself in the LEGO Dynamic Duo Funhouse Escape set.

4 The Joker once tricked Superman into aiding an Arkham Asylum breakout.

5 In the LEGO Dynamic Duo Funhouse Escape set, Joker has captured Batman.

6 The Joker's gun is firing a flag in the LEGO Batwing Battle over Gotham City set.

7 The Joker's hair is usually purple.

8 In the LEGO Arkham Asylum Breakout set, the Joker has restraints in the security van.

9 The Joker holds the record for incarcerations in Arkham Asylum.

10 The Joker is thought to have been the first Red Hood.

11 In the LEGO The Joker Bumper Car set, Joker is carrying a stick of dynamite.

12 The Joker got his scary clown-like appearance after falling into a vat of chemicals.

13 The Joker once escaped from Arkham Asylum by digging with a spoon.

14 Batman has a special Joker Protocol for all missions related to the Joker.

15 The Joker's nickname is the Funny Guy.

16 In the LEGO Dynamic Duo Funhouse Escape set, the Joker makes his getaway in a clown car.

17 The Joker has the power of super-strength.

18 The Joker once stole Bruce Wayne's Man of the Year award.

19 The Joker once came up with the idea of selling laughing-gas ice cream.

20 In the LEGO Batwing Battle Over Gotham City, Joker's helicopter is armed with a laughing-gas bomb.

21 The car in the LEGO The Joker Notorious Lowrider set has working suspension.

22 The Joker successfully teams up with Scarecrow to spread chaos and fear through Gotham City.

23 The Joker hires chemists to make his evil potions.

24 Joker Venom puts a smile on everyone's face.

25 The Joker is using a Penguin dummy for target practice in the LEGO The Joker Battle Training set.

MY EVIL PLOTS ARE NO JOKE!

26 The Joker's LEGO Notorious Lowrider has a golden clown hood ornament.

27 It is not a good idea to smell the flower that the Joker often wears on his jacket.

28 The Joker's Joy Buzzers are just a bit of fun.

29 The Joker and Poison Ivy are friends.

30 The Joker once drove a Jokermobile.

Answers on page 123 and 124

JOKERLAND

At first sight, Jokerland looks a whole lot of fun. But beware and be warned—this attraction is nothing like a normal funfair!

1 What is the name of Harley Quinn's scary bike ride?

a. Wheels of Fire
b. Terror Track
c. Motorcycle Madness
d. Harley's Horrorshow

2 Who is trapped underneath Harley Quinn's motorcycle?

a. Nightwing
b. Robin
c. Beast Boy
d. Batman

3 True or false?

These Batwing pieces have featured on two other LEGO Batmobiles.

4 True or false?

There are two sets of handcuffs in this set.

5 How many spring-loaded missiles does this Batmobile carry?

a. None   b. One   c. Two   d. Six

Jokerland (76035)

6 Which of these is the Joker's pie NOT likely to be?

a. Horrible
b. Home-made
c. Disgusting
d. Delicious

7 Which hero has Poison Ivy caught in her man-eating plant ride?

a. Raven
b. Supergirl
c. Starfire
d. Batgirl

8 True or false?

Poison Ivy is holding a long green rubber hose for watering plants.

9 What is inside the chamber at the bottom of the slide?

a. Slime
b. Poison
c. Spinach soup
d. Mouldy custard

10 True or false?

The Penguin brings two robot minions to Jokerland.

SHOOT 'O' MATIC

79

VILLAINOUS VEHICLES

Every super-villain needs a suitably scary-looking vehicle. As well as looking cool, it helps them to make a speedy getaway once the Super Heroes arrive on the scene!

1 Which marine animal is **BLACK MANTA'S SHIP STYLED TO LOOK LIKE?**

a. A manta ray
b. A shark
c. A starfish
d. A seahorse

2 How does Darkseid get around in the LEGO **DARKSEID INVASION** set?

a. By bicycle
b. On a hover platform
c. On a skateboard
d. On a pogo stick

3 Who finally convinced the Joker to give up his **JOKERMOBILE** as it was "too corny?"

a. Batman
b. Robin
c. Harley Quinn
d. Scarecrow

4 What is the name of **KILLER CROC'S** vehicle in the LEGO Batman: Killer Croc Sewer Smash set?

a. Bat-Tank
b. Battle Chomper
c. Crocmobile
d. Sewer Cycle

5 True or false?
Killer Moth's Mothmobile has antennae to sense danger.

6 What is the **RIDDLER'S** super-fast vehicle in the LEGO Batman: The Riddler Chase set?

a. Dragster
b. Jet ski
c. Spacecraft
d. Jet aircraft

Captain Boomerang

Killer Croc and his Battle Chomper

7 What decorates the front of the **JOKER'S STEAM ROLLER** in the LEGO Batman: The Joker Steam Roller set?

a. A picture of Harley Quinn
b. A joke gun
c. A flower squirting water
d. A giant smile

8 In the LEGO Catwoman: Catcycle City Chase set, what color is the **CATCYCLE?**

a. Black
b. Red
c. Purple
d. Green

9 What is **HARLEY QUINN** riding in the LEGO Dynamic Duo Funhouse Escape set?

a. A carousel horse
b. A roller coaster car
c. A ghost train
d. The Batmobile

10 In the LEGO Batwing Battle Over Gotham City set, what sort of **BOMB** is the Joker's helicopter carrying?

a. Laughing gas
b. Itching powder
c. Banana skins
d. Slime

11 In the LEGO Superman: Battle of Smallville set, what is the **NAME OF THE DROPSHIP** the evil Kryptonians use?

a. Kryptoship
b. Zodcopter
c. Black Zero
d. White One

12 Which villain drives **THE ICE CAR** in the LEGO Speed Force Freeze Pursuit set?

a. Captain Cold
b. Mr. Freeze
c. Killer Frost
d. The Penguin

13 What is the name of **LOBO'S VEHICLE** in the LEGO Superman & Krypto Team-Up set?

a. Super Dog
b. Killer Frog
c. Egg Nog
d. Space Hog

14 True or false? The Jokermobile was equipped with a giant boxing glove in the trunk.

15 Whose LEGO Mighty Micros vehicle features a **LARGE DRILL** mounted on the front?

a. Catwoman
b. Captain Cold
c. Bane
d. Killer Moth

16 In the LEGO Batboat Harbor Pursuit set, what is **DEATHSTROKE'S** mode of transport?

a. Jet ski
b. Row boat
c. Inflatable banana
d. Waterskis

GENIUS QUESTION

What unusual feature does Brainiac's skull-shaped star ship have?

81

CATWOMAN

This stealthy cat-burglar cannot resist other people's jewels. Batman often foils her crimes, but he still has a soft spot for Catwoman.

DIAMONDS ARE DEFINITELY THIS GIRL'S BEST FRIEND!

1 What is Catwoman's real name?

a. Pamela Isley
b. Harleen Quinzel
c. Caitlyn Snow
d. Selina Kyle

2 Catwoman's LEGO minifigures are mainly in black or which other color?

a. Gray
b. Blue
c. Purple
d. Red

3 True or false?
When Batman first meets Catwoman, he lets her escape from the scene of her crime.

4 Where does Catwoman live?

a. Coast City
b. Central City
c. Gotham City
d. Metropolis

5 What is Catwoman's nickname?

a. Kitty-Kitty
b. Princess of Plunder
c. The Dark Duchess
d. The Beautiful Burglar

6 What is Catwoman carrying for her LEGO Mighty Micros battle with Batman?

a. Fish
b. Milk
c. Energy drink
d. Cream pie

7 Catwoman is a skilled...?

a. Gymnast
b. Martial artist
c. Burglar
d. All of the above

GENIUS QUESTION
What is the name of Catwoman's favorite pet cat?

8 What is her signature weapon, carried in the LEGO Catwoman Catcycle City Chase set?

a. Cat o'nine tails whip

b. Catarang

c. Spear

d. Bow and arrow

9 Catwoman formed a team called the Gotham City Sirens—who else was in it?

a. Katana and Lady Shiva

b. Batgirl and Spoiler

c. Talia al Ghūl and Cheetah

d. Poison Ivy and Harley Quinn

10 Catwoman's most famous costume has ears and which other regular feature?

a. Cape

c. "C" symbol

b. Goggles

d. A tail

11 What is Catwoman's favorite mode of transport?

a. Motorcycle

c. Helicopter

b. Dragster

d. Sports car

12 True or false?

Catwoman knows that Batman is also billionaire Bruce Wayne.

13 What unusual feature does Catwoman's LEGO Mighty Micros vehicle have?

a. A drill

c. A tail

b. A snow plow

d. Exhaust flames

14 What is Catwoman stealing in the LEGO Catwoman Catcycle City Chase set?

a. Money

b. A diamond

c. A safe

d. Kryptonite

15 What feline weapon has Catwoman incorporated into her costume?

a. Clawed gloves

b. Whip-like tail

c. Razor-sharp whiskers

d. Fanged teeth

Catwoman

16 True or false?

Catwoman sometimes fights for good.

83

Answers on page 124

BAD BEASTS

These beastly types are anything but cuddly. Some of them even want to take over the world!

1 **True or false?** There are no bananas in the LEGO Gorilla Grodd Goes Bananas set.

2 **What is Man-Bat's weapon in the LEGO Batman: Man-Bat Attack set?**
a. A boomerang   c. Dynamite
b. A Batarang   d. A bow and arrow

3 **Which hapless villain once turned himself into a criminal version of Batman, complete with a special automobile?**
a. Man-Bat   c. Killer Croc
b. Gorilla Grodd   d. Killer Moth

4 **Which of these LEGO minifigures sports a cape?**
a. Gorilla Grodd   c. King Shark
b. The Penguin   d. Man-Bat

5 **Which beastly villain is based in Hawaii?**
a. Cheetah   c. Killer Croc
b. Man-Bat   d. King Shark

I'M GREEN, MEAN, BUT SELDOM SEEN!

6 **True or false?**
Cheetah's LEGO minifigure has the same hairpiece as Lois Lane.

7 **What is the name of Cheetah's alter ego?**
a. Barbara Minerva
b. Doris Zuel
c. Caitlin Snow
d. Pamela Isley

Killer Croc

3 What sort of animal is Dex-Starr, the Red Lantern?

a. Dog   b. Rabbit   c. Cat   d. Mouse

9 In the LEGO Killer Croc Sewer Smash set, Killer Croc carries which other villain on his vehicle?

a. The Penguin   c. Man-Bat
b. Captain Boomerang   d. Gorilla Grodd

10 What is Killer Croc's real name?

a. Kirk Langstrom   c. Waylon Jones
b. Oswald Cobblepot   d. Drury Walker

11 Is Man-Bat's weird mutation caused by...

a. Using an untested serum   c. Accidentally eating a bat
b. Drinking from Batman's cup   d. A misfiring magic spell

12 What color shorts does Killer Croc's LEGO bigfig wear?

a. Blue   b. Red   c. Green   d. Yellow

13 Why does Killer Croc look like a scaly reptile?

a. He lives in sewers   c. It's a genetic condition
b. He's half crocodile   d. It's just a costume

14 Where is Gorilla Grodd from?

a. Metropolis   c. Central City
b. Gotham City   d. Gorilla City

15 True or false?
Cheetah's main enemy is Batman.

GENIUS QUESTION

Which stripy, animal-like villain possesses magnetic powers?

16 Gorilla Grodd can speak to humans, but what other amazing power does he have?

a. Telepathy
b. X-ray vision
c. Super-speed
d. Flight

LEGO DC
UNIVERSE

Bizarro

I'M HOPING TO LAND A *WORLD-EXCLUSIVE!*

Lois Lane

Dr. Harleen Quinzel

Green Lantern's Power Battery

GOTHAM CITY

Gotham City is dark and gritty, full of crime and villainy. Fortunately, Batman and his Super Hero allies are on patrol to stop the bad guys taking over!

1 The hero featured in the LEGO Gotham City Cycle Chase is Batman.

2 Gotham City's main prison is called Whitegate Penitentiary.

3 The city's craziest crooks end up in Arkham Asylum.

4 The most dangerous part of Gotham City is called Crime Street.

5 When Batman takes a rare vacation, he leaves Gotham City in Wonder Woman's care.

6 The Legion of Doom sets up its Hall of Doom headquarters in Slaughter Swamp, just outside Gotham City.

7 Monstrous Solomon Grundy is usually found in Robinson Park.

8 The Joker gets his unique appearance following an accident at the King Chemical Processing Plant.

9 Wayne Manor is located in the center of Gotham City.

10 Batman's parents came from old Gotham City families who traditionally hated each other.

11 The headquarters of the Gotham City Police Department is in the Old Gotham district.

12 Poison Ivy once declared herself the ruler of Robinson Park.

13 The name of Gotham City's wealthiest area is the Gold District.

14 Gotham City descended into chaos when it was laid waste by an earthquake.

15 Wayne Tower is guarded by 12 gargoyles, called "guardians."

16 Gotham City is served by Archie Goodwin International Airport.

17 Bruce Wayne also owns the Wayne Foundation, which deals with his extensive charitable work.

18 The LEGO Clayface Splat Attack features a mayor of Gotham City.

19 The permanent carnival in north Gotham City is called Funhouse Esplanade.

20 Catwoman is from Gotham City's wealthiest district.

21 Both Bruce and Damian Wayne graduated from the elite school, Gotham Academy.

22 The *Gotham Gazette* is the city's major newspaper.

23 The Penguin runs his criminal operation from a Gotham City nightclub.

24 Underneath Gotham City is an abandoned highway system.

25 Batman has complete faith in the Gotham City Police Department.

26 Superman is not a fan of Gotham City.

27 Brainiac once shrank Gotham City to add it to his collection.

28 Several of Gotham City's villains have teamed up to defeat Superman, Wonder Woman, and Cyborg.

29 Gotham City, like New York City, has a Statue of Liberty in its harbor.

30 The most popular nightclub for Gotham City's criminals is called My Alibi.

METROPOLIS

This bustling city is home to Superman. It is also frequently the target of super-villains.

HI! I'M LOIS LANE, FROM THE *DAILY PLANET*. HOLD THE FRONT PAGE!

1 **What is the fruity nickname of Metropolis?**

a. The Big Apple

b. The Big Apricot

c. The Big Lemon

d. The Big Melon

2 **Which of these is NOT an area of Metropolis?**

a. Bakerline

b. Queensland Park

c. Hob's Bay

d. Lextown

3 **What is the name of the newspaper that Clark Kent and Lois Lane work for?**

a. The *Daily Bat*

b. *Super News*

c. The *Daily Planet*

d. The *Metropolis Times*

4 **What is the main road of the city of Metropolis called?**

a. Broad Street

b. Fifth Avenue

c. The Avenue of Tomorrow

d. Superman Boulevard

5 **Which minifigures are featured in the LEGO Superman: Metropolis Showdown set?**

a. Superman and Batman

b. Superman and Wonder Woman

c. Superman and General Zod

d. Lois Lane and Lex Luthor

6 **What is the Wonderland district of Metropolis best known for?**

a. Theaters

b. Cafes

c. Theme parks

d. Scientific research

7 **Who first used the name "Superman" to describe the new hero of Metropolis?**

a. Wonder Woman

b. Lois Lane

c. Batman

d. Lex Luthor

8 The Justice League's headquarters is in Metropolis. What is it called?

a. The Cottage of Justice
b. The Hall of Justice
c. The Tower of Justice
d. The Hut of Justice

13 What university did Clark Kent attend?

a. Super Tech
b. Metropolis University
c. Justice College
d. Harvard University

9 What vehicle features in the LEGO Superman: Metropolis Showdown set?

a. A boat
b. A rocket
c. A car
d. A helicopter

14 Which villain tries to steal the globe that sits atop the Daily Planet Building?

a. Catwoman
b. The Penguin
c. General Zod
d. Lex Luthor

10 There is a comics publisher based in Metropolis—what is its company name?

a. Crazy Comics
b. Gold Comics
c. Planet Comics
d. Blaze Comics

15 What is the tallest building in the city?

a. The LexCorp Tower
b. The Hall of Justice
c. The Daily Planet Building
d. Superman's house

11 How many Lex Luthor LEGO minifigures are there?

a. 1
b. 14
c. 40
d. 4

16 Which villain miniaturizes and bottles central Metropolis as part of an evil plot?

a. Lex Luthor
b. Brainiac
c. Doomsday
d. Darkseid

12 In the LEGO Superman: Metropolis Showdown set, how does General Zod try to defeat Superman?

a. Slipping him up on a banana peel
b. Trapping him under an antenna tower
c. Zapping him with a shrink ray
d. Firing Kryptonite at him

17 The golden Solar Tower skyscraper was briefly the HQ for which Super Hero team?

a. Teen Titans
b. Justice League
c. The Super Troopers
d. Justice League International

I VOW TO KEEP METROPOLIS SAFE FROM SUPER-VILLAINS!

Superman

TRUE OR FALSE?
KRYPTON

Krypton is Superman and Supergirl's home planet. Before it exploded, it was also the base of super-villains, such as General Zod, Tor-An, and Faora.

1 Krypton orbits a blue sun.

2 Krypton's capital city was Kandor.

3 Superman is from the city of Kandor.

4 Superman's parents are the King and Queen of Krypton.

5 Krypton has a radioactive core.

6 Kryptonians can fly on their home planet.

7 General Zod captures Lois Lane in the LEGO Superman: Battle of Smallville set.

8 The Jor-El minifigure shares his hairpiece with the Green Lantern minifigure.

9 The Earth's oxygen gives Kryptonians amazing powers.

10 The Kryptonian General Zod is Superman's uncle.

11 The LEGO Superman: Battle of Smallville set contains four Kryptonians.

12 Krypton's radioactive core causes the planet to be destroyed.

13 The material Kryptonite is invented by Brainiac to defeat Kryptonians like Superman.

14 Krypton is home to a creature called the thought-eating mole.

15 The villain Doomsday is from Krypton.

16 Krypton is destroyed in the year 50,000 of the Kryptonian calendar.

17 Supergirl appears in only one LEGO set.

18 Superman's mother is called Lara Lor-Van.

19 Kryptonite is toxic to Kryptonians like Superman.

20 The explosion of Krypton is visible from Earth 27 years later.

21 Superman's father is called Zor-El.

22 Nightwing takes his name from a Kryptonian legend.

23 Krypton has three moons.

24 Krypton is the only planet to orbit its sun.

25 There is a Kryptonian species similar to an Earth dog.

26 The bizarre Kryptonian thought-beast has a screen on its head.

27 The name of Krypton's sun is Rao.

28 There are no dangerous creatures on Krypton.

29 Kryptonians need to wear special armor when they first arrive on Earth.

30 The Tor-An minifigure wears blue armor.

31 Kryptonians are immortal.

32 Braniac saves 100,000 citizens of Kandor by shrinking the city.

I'VE GOT ALL THE POWERS OF SUPERMAN, BUT I'M NO HERO. ZOD'S THE NAME AND CONQUEST IS THE GAME!

General Zod

93

AROUND THE WORLD

Most places in the world have Super Heroes—as well as super-villains looking to cause trouble. When you're a hero, the whole of planet Earth is yours to protect!

GENIUS QUESTION

Which Canadian city is the explosive super-villain Plastique from?

1 Where is Captain Boomerang from?
a. France   **b.** Ireland   **c.** Canada   **d.** Australia

2 Batman's butler Alfred is originally from where?
a. USA   **b.** Scotland   **c.** U.K.   **d.** Canada

3 Which hero was originally from the African nation of Zambesi?
a. Vixen   **b.** Huntress   **c.** Mera   **d.** Hawkgirl

4 In which chilly location did Superman build his Fortress of Solitude?
a. Siberia   **b.** Alaska   **c.** Arctic   **d.** Antarctic

YOU CAN PROBABLY GUESS WHERE I'M FROM!

5 In the LEGO Batman: Killer Croc Sewer Smash set, what color are Captain Boomerang's boomerangs?
a. Red   **b.** Blue   **c.** Brown   **d.** Black

6 Blue Beetle Jaime Reyes is from Texas, but where were his parents born?
a. Mexico   **b.** Puerto Rico   **c.** Cuba   **d.** Guatemala

7 Where in the world is Lady Shiva from?
a. India   **c.** China
b. Japan   **d.** Korea

Captain Boomerang

8 Where did Azrael travel for his training from the Order of St. Dumas?

a. France   **c.** Belgium

b. Switzerland   **d.** Italy

9 Which British city is Barbara Minerva, alias Cheetah, from?

a. London   **c.** Liverpool

b. Nottingham   **d.** Sheffield

10 True or false?

Super Hero Black Lightning's home base is Chicago.

11 True or false?

Manchester Black has a tattoo of his national flag.

Cheetah

12 What is Green Arrow's home town?

a. Seattle   **c.** Metropolis

b. Paris   **d.** London

13 The young Bane was raised in a prison on the island of Santa Prisca. Where is Santa Prisca?

a. The Mediterranean Sea   **c.** The Pacific Ocean

b. The Caribbean Sea   **d.** The Indian Ocean

14 Gorilla City, home of Gorilla Grodd, is in which continent?

a. Europe   **b.** South America   **c.** Asia   **d.** Africa

15 As well as Paris and Pisa, which other European city does Brainiac manage to shrink?

a. Berlin   **b.** London   **c.** Madrid   **d.** Brussels

16 In which U.S. city did the Super Hero Shazam grow up?

a. Cleveland   **c.** Philadelphia

b. Pittsburgh   **d.** Boston

FAMILY

For heroes and villains, family is complicated. Sometimes they are the ones that have your back in a crisis, sometimes they're the ones causing the crisis!

GENIUS QUESTION
Which of Cyborg's family members created the tech that turned him into a metahuman?

1 What is the real name of Blackfire, Starfire's nemesis and sister?

a. Salamand'r   **b.** Komand'r   **c.** Alexand'r   **d.** Kamr'a

2 **True or false?** Batman's mother and Superman's adopted mother have the same first name.

3 What relation is Supergirl to Superman?

a. Sister   **b.** Niece   **c.** Cousin   **d.** Aunt

4 After Bruce Wayne's parents are killed, who acts as a father figure for the young orphan?

a. Wilfred   **b.** Alfred   **c.** Albert   **d.** Walter

5 What is the name of Superman's Kryptonian father?

a. Kal-El   **b.** Lar-El   **c.** Zor-El   **d.** Jor-El

6 Who is Batgirl's father?

a. Bruce Wayne   **c.** Dick Grayson
b. Commissioner Gordon   **d.** The Joker

7 What is the name of Rā's al Ghūl's daughter?

a. Barbara   **b.** Helena   **c.** Talia   **d.** Selina

8 Which Justice League member is Mera married to?

a. Aquaman   **c.** The Flash
b. Cyborg   **d.** Green Lantern

9 Which costumed hero is Batman's cousin?

a. Batgirl   **b.** Batwoman   **c.** Azrael   **d.** Huntress

10 What relation is Hippolyta to Wonder Woman?

a. Sister

b. Daughter

c. Mother

d. Aunt

11 What is the name of the shape-shifting alien Jayna's brother?

a. Van   c. Zan

b. Kan   d. Xan

12 True or false?

Darkseid sends his son Orion to live with his enemy, Highfather.

13 What is the name of Darkseid's other son?

a. Kalibak   c. Salirad

b. Kaliban   d. Lightseid

14 True or false?

Everybody from Lightning Lad's planet has a twin.

Supergirl

15 What relation is Aqualad to Aquaman?

a. Son   c. Cousin

b. Nephew   d. No relation

16 Which Teen Titan is the child of the demon called Trigon?

a. Starfire   c. Beast Boy

b. Raven   d. Robin

Lightning Lad

Answers on page 126

ANIMALS

The battles between Super Heroes and super-villains are not just fought by humanoids. Sometimes animals join in—on both sides!

GENIUS QUESTION

What animal is the power-ring-wielding Green Loontern?

1 Where is Krypto the Super-Dog from?

a. Kryptopolis
c. Kryptoville
b. Krypton
d. Smallville

2 What is the name of the cat in the Legion of Super-Pets?

a. Freaky
c. Streaky
b. Deaky
d. There isn't one

3 What is the name of Batman's son Damian's dog?

a. Rover
c. Titus
b. Spot
d. Fluffy

4 What type of creature appears in the LEGO Batman: Rescue from Rā's al Ghūl set?

a. Hippo
c. Scorpion
b. Lizard
d. Fish

5 What is the name of the rescue dog adopted by Bruce Wayne?

a. Chase the Bat-Hound
c. Buddy the Bat-Hound
b. Ace the Bat-Hound
d. Alf the Bat-Hound

6 What does the Bat-Hound wear to help him on crime-fighting missions?

a. Utility Collar
c. Utility Leash
b. Utility Coat
d. Utility Belt

7 True or false? Krypto can fly just like Superman.

8 Which animal comes in the LEGO Batman Classic TV Series—Batcave set?

a. Cat   b. Raccoon   c. Parrot   d. Chipmunk

9 Which member of the animal Bat-family is rescued by Damian Wayne?

a. Bat-Horse   b. Bat-Cat   c. Bat-Pig   d. Bat-Cow

10 Which canine companion appears in the LEGO Justice League Anniversary Party set?

a. Green Dog   c. Wonder Dog
b. Hawk Dog   d. Speedy Dog

11 What kind of animal is Superman's pet, Beppo?

a. Monkey   c. Lizard
b. Tortoise   d. Cat

12 Which super-villain transfers his mind into the body of an albino gorilla?

a. Crazy Quilt
b. Ultra-Humanite
c. Dr. Hugo Strange
d. Calendar Man

Krypto

13 True or false?   As well as Catwoman, there is a super-villain named Catman.

14 What sort of animal is The Flash's pet, named Whatzit?

a. Dog   b. Parrot   c. Cheetah   d. Turtle

15 What is the name of the Red Lantern who was formerly a beloved Earth pet?

a. Flet-Charr   b. Dex-Starr   c. Pheel-Ixx   d. Tee-Dells

16 True or false?   Beast Boy can change into a dinosaur.

TRUE OR FALSE?
ALIEN WORLDS

The universe is filled with weird and wonderful aliens and the planets they call home. But which aliens are friendly, and which are scary world-conquerors?

1 Wonder Woman is an alien.

2 On Cosmic Boy's home planet Braal, everyone has magnetic powers.

3 Super Hero Saturn Girl comes from Saturn.

4 Lightning Lad is from the planet Winath.

5 Starfire's planet is Oa.

6 All people from Starfire's planet can fly.

7 Green Lantern comes from the planet Oa.

8 Sinestro comes from the planet Korugar.

9 Sinestro's power ring was created on Oa.

10 The homeworld of the Indigo Tribe of power ring wielders is Blok.

11 No Earthlings feature in the LEGO Superman: Battle of Smallville set.

12 Black Manta is from Mars.

13 The home of the evil Darkseid is the fire-scarred planet Apokolips.

14 Brainiac comes from the planet Colu.

15 Natives of Planet Colu have blue skin.

16 Bat-Mite is not an alien from Batman's universe, but the strange reality of the 5th Dimension.

17 Wonder Woman's LEGO Mighty Micros battle is against an alien.

18 Doomsday comes from the planet Krypton.

19 Villain Steppenwolf is from Apokolips.

20 Star Sapphire charges her power ring on the planet Zamaron.

21 Apokolips is the source of the powerful Nth Metal.

22 The base of rage-fuelled Red Lantern Atrocitus is the planet Ysmault.

23 One of the Justice League's alien foes looks like a massive jellyfish.

24 Batman is suited up for space in the LEGO Green Lantern vs. Sinestro set.

25 Hawkman and Hawkgirl are both from the planet Thanagar.

I KNOW I LOOK SCARY, BUT I'M REALLY ONE OF THE GOOD GUYS!

26 Martian Manhunter hates any food that tastes sweet.

27 Super-villain Lobo is from the planet Czarnia.

28 A natural disaster wipes out everyone apart from Lobo on his homeworld.

Martian Manhunter

29 Super Heroes Jayna and Zan, from the planet Exor, are cousins.

30 Zan has the power to transform into anything water-related.

ROMANCE

Teaming up on nerve-wracking missions, it's no wonder that Super Heroes—and even super-villains—sometimes fall in love. But these fine romances rarely run smoothly!

1 Who is Superman's girlfriend?
a. Vicki Vale
b. Lois Lane
c. Selina Kyle
d. Merad

2 Who was Wonder Woman's first love?
a. Superman
b. Batman
c. Steve Trevor
d. Green Lantern

3 Other than "Mr. J," what is Harley Quinn's pet name for the Joker?
a. Puddin'
b. Sweetcheeks
c. Honeybun
d. Mr. Giggles

4 Which Super Hero has had a long, stormy romance with Black Canary?
a. Green Lantern
b. Nightwing
c. Green Arrow
d. Hawkman

5 Batman has had several serious (he's always serious!) relationships, but who is the mother of his son, Damian?
a. Catwoman
b. Vicki Vale
c. Zatanna
d. Talia al Ghūl

Batman

6 What is the name of Victor Fries's wife, who he is trying to save when he becomes Mr. Freeze?
a. Laura
b. Nora
c. Dora
d. Cora

7 Tim Drake has dated which of Gotham City's other guardians?
a. Batgirl
b. Huntress
c. Spoiler
d. Batwoman

8 True or false?

Star Sapphire has been Green Lantern Hal Jordan's boss and also dated him.

9 Who does Aquaman ask to be his Queen of Atlantis?

a. Starfire   b. Wonder Woman   c. Katana   d. Mera

10 Which Teen Titan has dated teammate Raven?

a. Kid Flash   b. Beast Boy   c. Cyborg   d. Robin

11 True or false?   Batman and Catwoman have never dated.

12 Who is futuristic hero Saturn Girl's boyfriend?

a. Lightning Lad   c. Superboy
b. Cosmic Boy   d. Booster Gold

13 Who is Dick Grayson's girlfriend?

a. Vicki Vale   c. Supergirl
b. Barbara Gordon   d. Wonder Woman

14 Which Teen Titan is the boyfriend of Terra, before she betrays the team?

a. Cyborg   c. Beast Boy
b. Robin   d. Kid Flash

Catwoman

15 True or false?

Hawkman and Hawkgirl are boyfriend and girlfriend.

16 Who was Clark Kent's first girlfriend in Smallville?

a. Laura Lee
b. Lana Lang
c. Lori Lemaris
d. Lyla Lerroll

GENIUS QUESTION

What grand romantic gesture did Harley Quinn make for the Joker in Arkham Asylum?

103

Answers on page 126

CAREERS

Sometimes even heroes and villains need a day job. Some of them work in the media, some in the police force, and some (usually the bad guys!) are scientists.

1 What is **CLARK KENT'S** job when he's not being Superman?

a. Accountant
b. Newspaper reporter
c. Radio DJ
d. Coffee barista

2 Barry Allen, The Flash, is a **SCIENTIST** in what sort of workplace?

a. Crime laboratory
b. University
c. Research facility
d. Museum

3 What job did the shape-shifting villain **CLAYFACE** hold in the past?

a. Police officer
b. Magician
c. Actor
d. Firefighter

4 Killer Croc used to work for a **CARNIVAL** —as what?

a. Ticket seller
b. Ferris wheel operator
c. Fortune teller
d. Wrestler

5 What was Green Lantern **HAL JORDAN'S JOB?**

a. Pilot
b. Miner
c. Train driver
d. Construction worker

6 True or false? Batman's butler Alfred was once an actor.

7 Poison Ivy Pamela Isley is notorious as a super-villain with **PLANT-BASED POWERS,** but she started out as a...

a. Doctor
b. Architect
c. Garden designer
d. Botanist

TRUST ME, I'M A DOCTOR!

Harleen Quinzel

8 Before she became Harley Quinn, what was Harleen Quinzel's job at

ARKHAM ASYLUM?

a. Psychiatrist **c.** Security guard

b. Cook **d.** Nurse

9 Unfortunately, some people choose to take jobs as

HENCHMEN

for villains. Who does this henchman work for?

a. Two-Face **c.** Mr. Freeze

b. Penguin **d.** The Joker

10 And which **VILLAIN** employs this henchman?

a. Two-Face

b. Penguin

c. Mr. Freeze **d.** The Joker

11 What role does the **FEARSOME ARKILLO** have in the Sinestro Corps?

a. Drill sergeant **c.** Yoga instructor

b. Cleaner **d.** Sinestro's butler

12 Which one of these does NOT fall into the category

"MAD SCIENTIST"?

a. Pamela Isley (Poison Ivy)

b. Jonathan Crane (Scarecrow)

c. Leonard Snart (Captain Cold)

d. Victor Fries (Mr. Freeze)

13 True or false? The super-villain Firefly used to be a firefighter.

14 Which of these characters does NOT own a **BILLION-DOLLAR CORPORATION?**

a. Nightwing **c.** Green Arrow

b. Batman **d.** Lex Luthor

15 Which award-winning **REPORTER** is quickly on the scene with a camera in the LEGO Heroes of Justice: Sky High Battle set?

a. Jimmy Olsen **c.** Lois Lane

b. Clark Kent **d.** Vicki Vale

16 Which hero has a day job in her family's

FLOWER SHOP?

a. Katana

b. Black Canary

c. Batgirl

d. Poison Ivy

GENIUS QUESTION

Which hero is also a successful stage magician?

ROBOTS

More than just machines, some robots have a life of their own. But which ones are heroes or allies, and which ones want to destroy humanity?

1 Which member of the Justice League is mostly made of machine parts?

a. Cyborg
b. Batman
c. The Flash
d. Martian Manhunter

2 Cyborg has robot duplicates. What are they called?

a. Stonetrons   b. Borgbots   c. Mini Cys   d. Cybots

3 As well as Cyborg, which other Justice League Super Hero has built robot duplicates of himself?

a. Batman
b. Superman
c. The Flash
d. Green Lantern

4 In the LEGO Gorilla Grodd Goes Bananas set, the Bat-Mech is armed with two stud shooters and...

a. A banana shooter
b. A Kryptonite gun
c. A net shooter
d. Mallet hands

5 True or false?
Penguin uses penguin robots to cause chaos and even blow things up!

6 Which of these Superman enemies is NOT a robot, android, or cyborg?

a. Brainiac
b. Metallo
c. Cyborg Superman
d. Doomsday

I'M A SUPER-CLEVER SUPER-VILLAIN—AND I'M SUPER-ANGRY!

Brainiac

7 True or False?
The robot Brainiac was built to catalog every planet in the Universe.

8 Which of Superman's enemies has made robot copies of himself to fool the Man of Steel?

a. Toyman   **b.** Bizarro   **c.** Mr. Mxyzptlk   **d.** Lex Luthor

9 What are the Penguin's robots holding in the LEGO Batman: The Penguin Face Off set?

a. Diamonds   **b.** Dynamite   **c.** Fish   **d.** Bananas

10 Booster Gold's helpful robot companion, Skeets, comes from which century?

a. 18th   **b.** 20th   **c.** 35th   **d.** 25th

11 In the LEGO Black Manta Deep Sea Strike set, Black Manta has a robot shaped like a...

a. Sea horse   **b.** Shark   **c.** Starfish   **d.** Swordfish

12 What is Black Manta's robot armed with?

a. Harpoons   **c.** Stud shooters
b. Laser shooters   **d.** Net shooters

13 Which robot, created to destroy the Justice League, ends up a hero?

a. Red Tiger   **c.** Red Tornado
b. Red Terror   **d.** Red Tomato

14 Metallo's body is powered by...

a. Petroleum gas   **c.** Kryptonite
b. Coal   **d.** Omega Beams

GENIUS QUESTION

What is the robot identity adopted by U.S. Army Sergeant John Corben?

15 True or false?
Cyborg's head can lift away from his body and move around.

16 What color is Brainiac's head?

a. Blue
b. Gray
c. Green
d. Red

Answers on page 127

ATLANTIS

Aquaman is the king of the undersea realm of Atlantis, using his power over sea creatures to protect his people.

1 True or false?

A Parademon's wings are just for flight.

2 True or false?

The Parademon in this set is equipped with a Super Jumper.

3 Which other LEGO set contains this Parademon minifigure?

a. Knightcrawler Tunnel Attack
b. Flying Fox: Batmobile Airlift Attack
c. Black Manta Deep Sea Strike
d. Darkseid Invasion

4 This green plant piece is also used in the Arkham Asylum set to hang outside whose cell?

a. The Joker
b. The Riddler
c. Poison Ivy
d. Two-Face

Battle of Atlantis (76085)

5 True or false?

The Atlantean Guard minifigure is exclusive to this set.

6 How many Atlantean Guards fight by Aquaman's side in this set?

a. One
b. Two
c. Three
d. Four

7 True or false?

According to legend, Atlantis used to be above the sea.

8 What is the name of Aquaman's weapon?

a. Trident
b. Fork
c. Spiker
d. Ouch-Maker

9 Which villain has sent the Parademons to steal the Mother Box from Atlantis?

a. Sinestro
b. Steppenwolf
c. Lex Luthor
d. Black Manta

109

CLONES AND DISGUISES

Villains with a skill for science try to gain an edge by making clones of themselves, or even of their heroic enemies! However, on some secret missions, bad guys—and good guys— simply go in disguise...

Bizarro

1 Superboy is a clone combining DNA from which two people?

a. Superman and Lois
b. Batman and Supergirl
c. Superman and Doomsday
d. Superman and Lex Luthor

2 Which secretive scientific organization created Superboy?

a. The Clone Company
b. Doppelganger Inc.
c. Project Cadmus
d. D.O.U.B.L.E. Labs

3 Who creates Bizarro, using a duplicator ray?

a. Brainiac
b. Scarecrow
c. Prankster
d. Lex Luthor

4 What is Superboy's Kryptonian name?

a. Kon-El   c. Mon-An
b. Kal-L   d. Son-Al

5 Who is Bizarro a clone of?

a. Martian   c. Hawkman
   Manhunter   d. Green Arrow
b. Superman

6 Who creates Batzarro, an imperfect clone of Batman?

a. The Riddler   c. Toyman
b. The Joker   d. Ultra-Humanite

7 What is Bizarro's LEGO Mighty Micros vehicle equipped with?

a. A drill   c. Giant fists
b. A plow   d. Stud shooters

8 Brainiac creates a clone of himself in order to perform which particular job?

a. Emptying the trash

b. Making coffee

c. Defeating Superman

d. Assisting in a laboratory

9 What color is the suit worn by the LEGO Batzarro minifigure?

a. Black   c. Blue

b. Grey   d. Purple

10 Who is the alter ego of the master of disguise known as the Question?

a. Miss Terry   c. Edward Nigma

b. Charles Szasz   d. Jack Puzzle

11 Shape-shifter Martian Manhunter spends time on Earth disguised as a detective called...?

a. Jim James   c. John Jones

b. Jeff Jordan   d. Jed Jackett

12 Batman goes undercover by assuming a disguise and criminal identity—what is it?

a. Matches Malone

b. Crusher Corbett

c. Shorty O'Dowd

d. Slam Bradley

13 What does Batzarro declare himself to be?

a. The World's Greatest Clone

b. The World's Worst Detective

c. The Caped Clone

d. The Light Knight

14 The first time Batman stops Catwoman stealing a diamond, she is disguised as...?

a. An old lady   c. A man

b. A cat   d. Batman

15 True or false?
Clayface can transform into any shape he wishes.

16 True or false?
Superman uses different body language as Clark Kent to makes his disguise more convincing.

GENIUS QUESTION
Which Super Hero is able to take on the shape of any object, and even change his density?

TIME TRAVEL AND MIND CONTROL

Controlling people's minds, or whizzing backward or forward in time, may seem incredible powers—but they are easy for some Super Heroes and super-villains!

GENIUS QUESTION
Which member of the Legion of Super-Heroes has the power of mind control?

1 Which member of the Justice League travels through time on the Cosmic Treadmill?

a. Superman   **b.** Batman   **c.** Green Lantern   **d.** The Flash

2 While stuck in the future, where does Batman go to find equipment to help Superman?

a. The Fortress of Solitude   **c.** The Batcave
b. The Hall of Justice   **d.** Gotham City Police Headquarters

3 On one occasion, Batman has to rescue Wonder Woman from which other time?

a. Medieval times   **c.** Ancient Egyptian times
b. Cavemen times   **d.** Ancient Roman times

I KNOW WHAT YOU'RE THINKING!

4 A LEGO Batman minifigure shows Batman on a time-traveling adventure dressed as what?

a. Pirate   **c.** Cowboy
b. Roman soldier   **d.** Knight

5 Which hero has traveled to our time from the future?

a. Martian Manhunter   **c.** Doctor Fate
b. John Stewart   **d.** Booster Gold

6 True or false?
Super-villain Doctor Destiny is a time-traveling menace.

Brainiac

7 The super-villain Pied Piper is a musical mind-controller. What instrument does he use?

a. A tuba　　　　　c. A trumpet

b. A saxophone　　d. A flute

8 Which Super Hero can travel through time?

a. Kid Flash　　　c. Black Canary

b. Wonder Woman　d. Plastic Man

9 True or false?
Evil scientist Ultra-Humanite can put thoughts into people's minds.

10 True or false?
Martian Manhunter is famous for his time-traveling powers.

11 Which Justice League member is immune to Martian Manhunter's mind control?

a. Cyborg　　　c. Batman

b. Superman　　d. Wonder Woman

12 Which villain possesses mind-control technology?

a. Clayface　　c. Mad Hatter

b. Bane　　　　d. Two-Face

Gorilla Grodd

13 Which Super Hero team travels in time from the 30th century?

a. Justice League　　　c. Green Lantern Corps

b. Legion of Super-Heroes　d. Birds of Prey

14 Which villain uses a question-mark cane to confuse or even control his opponents' minds?

a. The Penguin　b. The Joker　c. The Riddler　d. Trickster

15 Which of these alien super-villains specializes in mind control?

a. Darkseid　　b. Brainiac　　c. Sinestro　　d. Doomsday

16 What piece of equipment boosts Gorilla Grodd's telepathic powers?

a. His helmet　　b. His shield　　c. His mask　　d. His gloves

Answers on page 127

MYSTERIOUS ARTIFACTS

Some Super Heroes and super-villains use magical objects to increase their power. In the wrong hands, these mysterious objects can be very dangerous!

1 What is the secret of Rā's Al Ghūl's **IMMORTALITY,** as featured in the LEGO Batman: Rescue from Ra's al Ghul set?

a. Eating raw vegetables
b. Lifting Weights
c. Using Moisturizer
d. Bathing in a Lazarus Pit

 Which Greek god made Wonder Woman's magical **LASSO OF TRUTH?**

a. Ares
b. Hephaestus
c. Zeus
d. Hades

 What is the most **POWERFUL ITEM** that Doctor Fate wears?

a. His helmet
b. His amulet
c. His cloak
d. His ring

4 Which villain uses the mind-controlling **PSYCHE STONE** to create his own army?

a. The Joker
b. Bane
c. Mr. Freeze
d. Penguin

5 Which **POWERFUL OBJECT** appears in the LEGO Superman vs. Power Armor Lex set?

a. Lasso of Truth
b. Mother Box
c. Helmet of Fate
d. Father Box

6 What is the name of Katana's **ENCHANTED SWORD?**

a. Longclaw
b. Sliceblade
c. Soultaker
d. Emmett

7 Rā's al Ghūl uses magic to **INCREASE HIS LIFESPAN.** How old is he?

a. 300 years
b. 450 years
c. 500 years
d. 600 years

8 Which magical object helps Aquaman command the **SEVEN SEAS?**

a. Trident of Poseidon
b. Spear of Neptune
c. Helmet of Zeus
d. Harpoon of Hermes

9 What are
BATMAN AND THE FLASH
trying to reach in the LEGO Knightcrawler Tunnel Attack set?

a. Lasso of Truth   c. Mother Box
b. Helmet of Fate   d. Psyche Stone

10 What is a
MOTHER BOX?

a. A useful storage container
b. A building block
c. A throwing weapon
d. A sentient computer

11 # WHERE do
Mother Boxes come from?

a. The planet Oa
b. The planet New Genesis
c. The planet Krypton
d. The planet Korugar

12 Mother Boxes enable a person to
TELEPORT
anywhere in the universe by means of...

a. Zoom tubes   c. Boom tubes
b. Loom tubes   d. Doom tubes

13 True or false?
On the planet Apokolips there is a dark version of a Mother Box called a Father Box.

14 Which
JUSTICE LEAGUE
member is tuned into the inner workings of Mother Boxes?

a. Cyborg   c. The Flash
b. Superman   d. Wonder Woman

15 Darkseid's son Orion uses a special
HARNESS
called the A4 that enables him to...

a. Teleport   c. Fire energy beams
b. Fly   d. All of the above

16 True or false?
The Central Power Battery on the planet Oa powers the rings of all Red Lanterns.

GENIUS QUESTION
Which color power ring is fueled by the emotion of hope?

Green Lantern's Power Battery

Answers on page 127

ANSWERS

WONDER WOMAN

1) b. Diana
2) b. Sword
3) a. Amazons
4) c. 6
5) False—she is the daughter of king of the gods, Zeus.

6) a. Paradise Island
7) a. Hippolyta
8) b. Ares
9) c. Steve Trevor
10) a. Invisible Jet
11) d. Tell the truth

12) d. X-ray vision
13) b. Justice League
14) a. Bracelets
15) d. Cheetah
Genius Question: Mexican food

SUPERMAN

1) b. Earth's yellow sun
2) b. Magic
3) True—the head is double-sided to show red "heat vision" eyes.
4) c. Smallville
5) a. Farmers
6) True
7) d. Kal-El

8) True—although in space he can fly even faster.
9) c. Green Kryptonite.
10) True—rather than being an Earth letter, the symbol represents the El family, and means 'hope'.
11) b. Man of Steel
12) a. Lex Luthor

13) a. Lead
14) True—trying to bite Superman can cause vampires to explode!
15) b. Supergirl
16) d. Faora
Genius Question: *To Kill a Mockingbird*

BATMAN

1) True— Batman uses his brilliant mind and martial arts skills to fight crime.
2) b. Man of Steel
3) b. Harpoon
4) c. The Bat-Signal

5) d. Gotham City
6) a. Robin
7) d. Batwing
8) a. Harley Quinn
9) c. Damian
10) b. Cyborg

11) c. Blue
12) True
13) b. Batcopter
14) d. A bat-symbol
15) d. Batman of Zurr-En-Arrh
16) b. Lucius Fox
17) d. The Rogues Gallery
Genius Question: Zorro

FLYING FOX

1) c. Heat vision
2) False—it is his uncle, Steppenwolf.
3) True—the Apokoliptians plan to use them to make Earth just like their fiery homeworld.

4) b. An eagle
5) a. Tactical suit
6) d. Batman
7) True—his blaster is built into his robotic arm.

8) True—so Batman's ride can get right to the heart of the action!
9) d. Three
10) b. One

BATMAN'S GADGETS

1) True—he uses them to create a diversion and confuse enemies.
2) True
3) False—he has a sword and a flail.
4) False—it is the Batcomputer.
5) True—they are one of Batman's favorite weapons.

6) False—it is white, to camouflage him in the snow.
7) False—it is used by the police to tell Batman they need him.
8) True—the equipment is part of his Space Batman outfit.
9) False—although he does carry smoke capsules.

10) True—his Bat-Mech suit gives him extra armor when facing powerful enemies.
11) False—it is a grappling hook gun.
12) True—the information helps him on future missions.
13) True—It helps him stay cool

in the harsh desert conditions.
14) False—Batman can summon the Batmobile via remote control.
15) True
16) False—it sprays tear gas at anyone trying to remove Batman's mask.
17) True—he likes to keep them within reach.
18) False—its compartments are locked and only Batman can open them.
19) True—he can use it to take fingerprints and safely bag

evidence.
20) True—the villain used an orange lightbulb to complete the effect.
21) False—it is a scuba suit.
22) True—Batman also has barracuda, manta ray, and whale repellents.
23) True—they are used for blasting through walls, not for hurting people.
24) True—The heroes fight against each other in this set.
25) False—he has linked it to the Batmobile to access it

on the go.
26) True—the Suit of Sorrows made him stronger and faster, but also made him do bad things.
27) False—there is no such Batarang.
28) True
29) True—Batman knew that the heat would dry Clayface into dust!
30) True—he uses it to interrogate villains.

PAGES 16–17
BAT-FAMILY

1) d. Batgirl
2) d. Adopted son
3) a. Nightwing
4) d. Red
5) c. Nightwing
6) b. Batarang
7) d. Commissioner Gordon

8) d. Red Hood
9) b. Boy Wonder
10) True—Batman is often so busy fighting crime that he forgets to eat healthily!
11) False—Kate Kane is Batman's cousin
12) d. Grapple-hook gun

13) b. Yellow
14) b. Batgirl and Robin
15) c. The Joker
16) True—both have red hair.
17) d. Supergirl
Genius Question: Bruce's parents, Thomas and Martha.

PAGES 18–19
THE FLASH

1) b. Barry Allen
2) a. The Fastest Man Alive
3) c. The Speed Force
4) a. Kid Flash
5) c. Forensic scientist
6) b. He was splashed with chemicals and then struck by

lightning.
7) d. Central City
8) True—he can travel through time using the Cosmic Treadmill.
9) True—but it was close!
10) c. Batman
11) d. Iris West

12) a. Sultan of Spin
13) c. Super-fast healing
14) d. Reverse-Flash
15) a. His own wifi hotspot
16) a. Captain Cold
17) b. An energy drink

PAGES 20–21
JUSTICE LEAGUE

1) True
2) True—it is the same as Superman's.
3) True—although he likes to do these things anyway.
4) True—his father was a human.
5) True—Superman, Batman, Wonder Woman, The Flash, Green Lantern, Martian Manhunter, and Aquaman.
6) True—he is from Thanagar.
7) False—he can breathe both on land and underwater.
8) False—Black Canary is Green Arrow's girlfriend.
9) True — The ring must be charged regularly using a Green Power Battery.

10) False—Cyborg never takes his suit off.
11) True
12) True
13) True—Batman also voted for himself!
14) False—she is the only one.
15) False—there are two.
16) False—it was Eel.
17) True—he uses this feature in space to combat the lack of gravity.
18) False—Green Lantern's energy comes from his willpower.
19) False—it comes from Nth Metal.
20) False—the Watchtower is a satellite headquarters orbiting Earth.

21) True
22) True—he can communicate telepathically with them.
23) False—the League was formed to protect the Earth.
24) True—its name was Starro.
25) True
26) True
27) False
28) True
29) True—his archery skills are not a superpower, just amazing talent and training!
30) True—they fight one another in the LEGO Batman vs. Superman Clash of the Heroes set.

PAGES 22-23
TEEN TITANS

1) d. A banana
2) b. Cyborg
3) c. Pink
4) True—her raven form can help her in battle.
5) b. A demon
6) a. Starfire

7) c. White
8) d. Nightwing
9) d. From an untested antidote after an animal bite.
10) c. Koriand'r
11) c. San Francisco
12) a. Circus acrobats

13) b. Kissing a human
14) a. Gar Logan
15) a. The Doom Patrol
16) a. Superman and Hawkman

Genius Question: Clock King

PAGES 24-25
WEIRD AND WONDERFUL

1) a. They're not, but she's still learning how to use them.
2) c. He was struck by lightning while covered in chemicals.
3) a. Blue Beetle
4) d. Katana
5) a. Brainiac
6) d. 30th

7) b. Black Canary
8) a. Huntress
9) b. Heat vision
10) c. Booster Gold
11) True—she is really a White Martian. She just chooses to appear green.
12) False—she is from the

rival kingdom of Xebel.
13) c. Doctor Fate
14) b. Starfire
15) **Picture Round:** B is Beast Boy
16) True—one alter ego is the physical body of Firestorm, the other offers advice.

Genius Question: Zatanna

PAGES 26-27
ALTER EGOS

1) True—Bruce then changes into one of three Batsuits to fight the Penguin.
2) False—Harvey becomes Two-Face after being scarred with acid.
3) True
4) True—after being wounded by the Joker, she aids the war on crime as Oracle.
5) False—Clark's high school sweetheart, Lana Lang, also knows his true identity.
6) True
7) False
8) False—Barry studied organic chemistry and minored in criminology.

9) False—Arthur Curry's father was a lighthouse keeper.
10) True—Kara, a.k.a. Supergirl, is Superman's cousin from Krypton.
11) True
12) True
13) True
14) False
15) False—she is his daughter.
16) False
17) True—but Shazam's magic turns Billy into a strong adult!
18) False—she uses technology to fight crime.
19) True—she later relocated to the U.S.
20) False—she is Black

Canary's alter ego.
21) True—he is a science professor who studies shrinking.
22) True—the daughter of a crime family, she has become a Super Hero.
23) False
24) True—at first she could not control her Star Sapphire power.
25) False—It is Rachel Roth.
26) True
27) True
28) False
29) True
30) False

PAGES 28-29
ALLIES

1) b. Alfred Pennyworth
2) d. Commissioner Gordon
3) d. Jimmy Olsen
4) c. Krypto
5) b. Reporter
6) c. Joanne

7) a. Perry White
8) c. Gotham City Police Department
9) True
10) c. Tray
11) a. Steve Trevor
12) a. British

13) c. Lois Lane
14) True
15) c. The Joker
16) Picture Round: C is Lois Lane.
Genius Question: He's an army officer.

PAGES 30-31
POWERS

1) a. The Flash
2) d. Batman
3) d. Superman
4) b. Shazam!
5) False—he can transform into any animal he has ever seen.
6) d. Green Lantern

7) c. Wonder Woman
8) b. Cyborg
9) True
10) a. Plastic Man
11) c. Magnetism
12) False—she has to speak it backward, "Gorf!"

13) b. Firestorm
14) True
15) Picture Round: D. Hawkman.
16) d. Martian Manhunter
Genius Question:
The ability to shrink.

PAGES 32-33
HIDDEN TALENTS

1) a. Painting
2) b. Chili
3) a. Black Canary
4) a. Dancing
5) d. Batman
6) c. Upgrading technology
7) d. The Flash
8) True—among other beasts, she has a dragon, a winged horse, and a sphinx.
9) a. The Batusi
10) b. Roses
11) c. Acrobatics
12) Picture Round:
    a. Green Lantern
13) False—Robin's circus background also gives him training in escapology.
14) d. Chess
15) c. A ping-pong table
16) d. Harmonica
Genius Question: Football

PAGES 34-35
WEAKNESSES

1) False—Kryptonite can be several colors, each with a different effect on Kryptonians.
2) True
3) False
4) True
5) True
6) False—it has appeared in 14 sets to date.
7) False—his main weakness is dehydration.
8) False—it is yellow, the color worn by his enemy Sinestro.
9) True
10) True
11) True
12) False—Nth Metal gives him his powers.
13) False—Green Kryptonite is toxic to all Kryptonians.
14) True
15) False—she is vulnerable to lead.
16) True—a lightning strike can turn him back into Billy Batson.
17) True
18) True
19) False—it is his bad temper!
20) True
21) True
22) True—it is Blue Kryptonite, harmless to Superman.
23) True
24) False—the ring must be regularly charged.
25) True
26) True
27) False—gas attacks are his weakness.
28) True
29) True
30) True—she once thought garden gnomes were statues of famous humans!

PAGES 36-37
TRAINING

1) b. A dojo
2) c. Madame Mantis
3) a. Deathstroke
4) b. A desert island
5) True—she did not want her mother to find out she was training to be a Super Hero.
6) d. None
7) d. Green Arrow
8) d. All of the above
9) b. Batman
10) True
11) c. Wonder Woman
12) a. Samurai
13) c. Miss Martian
14) d. Nightwing
15) a. Escapology
Genius Question: When he was in the British army.

PAGES 38-39
HERO VEHICLES

1) d. Green Arrow
2) d. Batman
3) b. A Car
4) c. Knightcrawler
5) b. A Jet
6) a. Batwing
7) b. Javelin
8) b. Motorcycle
9) a. Redbird Cycle
10) c. Nightwing
11) d. Flying Fox
12) d. Invisible Jet
13) b. CyborgCopter
14) a. Blue
15) c. The Bug
16) True
Genius Question: Pilot

PAGES 40-41
HIDEOUTS

1) b. Behind a grandfather clock
2) a. Wayne Manor
3) a. Batcopter
4) c. A parademon
5) b. A robotic penguin
6) c. Hall of Justice
7) True—it is a robot,
a memento of Batman's mission to Dinosaur Island.
8) a. Bottled City of Kandor
9) a. Robin
10) d. The letter T
11) b. Chicken goujons fried in olive oil
12) b. The rocket that carried Superman to Earth.
13) c. Fortress of Solitude
14) d. In Earth's orbit
15) d. Doctor Fate
16) a. Sub Diego
Genius Question: a. The Joker

COSTUMES

1) c. Batman
2) d. Superman
3) b. Green Lantern
4) a. The Flash
5) b. Wonder Woman
6) a. Superman
7) d. Cyborg
8) b. Hawkman
9) a. Aquaman
10) b. Raven and Starfire
11) c. Katana
12) c. Cyborg
13) a. Martian Manhunter
14) True
15) c. Batgirl
16) c. Yellow
Genius Question: Shazam!

BANANA BATTLE

1) a. Spring-loaded missiles
2) True
3) d. Devastating Ice Shooter
4) d. Four
5) True
6) c. Net
7) c. Gorilla Grodd
8) True
9) a. One
10) True

HERO TECHNOLOGY

1) c. Cream pie arrow
2) d. Blaster
3) a. Kryptonite blaster
4) True
5) a. In a ring he wears
6) c. Power Blast energy drink
7) True—the human part of Cyborg can even apparently die, and his tech will bring him back.
8) d. Dwarf stars
9) a. Red
10) b. Two grappling hooks
11) d. Fireworks arrow
12) b. Gas mask
13) False—his armor is created by the advanced tech in his alien scarab.
14) a. The Reach
15) b. A white noise cannon
16) b. "Slideways teleporter"
Genius Question: S.T.A.R. Labs

BATCAVE

1) c. Batcopter
2) d. Catwoman
3) b. Robin
4) True—they are usually black or gray!
5) b. Thomas and Martha Wayne
6) c. Commissioner Gordon
7) a. The button that opens the Batcave entrance
8) True—Batman can summon them using a special gadget.
9) True—and a Dick Grayson minifigure, too!
10) d. Joker Venom

ORIGIN STORIES

1) False—Superman comes from Planet Krypton.
2) False—it was Kansas.
3) False—he comes from Earth.
4) True—in order to block his heat vision.
5) False—he chose it to scare bad guys.
6) False—Bruce became Batman after his parents were killed.
7) True
8) False—he was given robotic body parts after an accident.
9) True
10) False—they were gifts from the Olympian Gods.
11) False
12) True—her name was Dr. Harleen Quinzel.
13) True—as an orphan, Bruce saw a kindred spirit in the boy.
14) True
15) False—he lived in Amnesty Bay, Maine.
16) False—but she now has resistance to all toxins.
17) True
18) True
19) True
20) True
21) True
22) False—she was already a highly trained martial artist.
23) True
24) False—he can only survive underwater in his high-tech suit.
25) True
26) True
27) True
28) True—because of his ability to face his fears.
29) False—his father owned a bird shop.
30) False—he took the name as it was an old identity of the Joker.

PAGES 54–55
CRAZY CROOKS

1) c. Black and red
2) a. A safe
3) a. Fear gas
4) b. Harley Quinn
5) a. Batman
6) d. Question marks

7) d. Biplane
8) c. Jonathan Crane
9) True—to make a getaway more fun!
10) b. The Riddler
11) a. Harley Quinn

12) c. Plants
13) b. Flips a coin
14) c. Anti-gravity boots
15) d. Pitchfork
16) a. The Mad Hatter
Genius Question: Harvey Dent

PAGES 56–57
ARKHAM ASYLUM

1) a. Bat-Signal
2) c. Harleen Quinzel
3) True—it has restraints for Batman's most dangerous foe, although he seems to have escaped!

4) True—and why not? He's Batman!
5) d. Fourteen
6) b. Monocle
7) True—the floral felon is one of Arkham's regulars!

8) d. It has a glow-in-the-dark head
9) a. Elizabeth Arkham, the founder's mother
10) False—it is a kendo staff.

PAGES 58–59
ALIEN TERRORS

1) d. General Zod
2) b. Green Lantern's battery
3) a. Yellow
4) b. Fear
5) d. Red
6) c. Parademons

7) c. Lobo
8) False—they cannot harm Doomsday, the ultimate survivor.
9) b. Space dolphin
10) c. Wonder Woman
11) b. Superman

12) a. Desaad
13) d. Sinestro Corps
14) a. Steppenwolf
15) c. Greed
16) a. Atrocitus
Genius Question: Steppenwolf

PAGES 60–61
THE WEIRD AND THE DEADLY

1) c. Ares
2) a. Deathstroke
3) a. Vandal Savage
4) b. Martial Arts
5) d. Clayface
6) b. Floyd Lawton
7) c. Mr. Mxyzptlk
8) a. Zombie

9) a. Monday
10) d. Gang boss
11) c. Gentleman Ghost
12) b. Deathstroke
13) b. Rocket launcher
14) c. Lady Shiva
15) False—at normal size she has a brilliant mind, but her

brainpower decreases as she gets larger.
16) False—it's Slade Wilson.
Genius Question: The Injustice Society

PAGES 62–63
ARCHENEMIES

1) True—although Wonder Woman just wants to be friends!
2) False—although he is not fond of the evil alien, Lex Luthor is his main enemy.
3) False—although the rest of his Rogues Gallery keep him busy, the Joker is his archenemy.
4) False—Bane is a bigfig.
5) True
6) True—the villainous Reverse-Flash.

7) True.
8) False—they are heroic allies.
9) True—their animosity has carried over from Dick Grayson's Teen Titans days.
10) True—he decided to try and defeat Oracle by supplying information to the villains she tracked.
11) False—her nemesis is her sister, Blackfire, cruel ruler of their home planet.

12) True—Sinestro was Hal Jordan's mentor before he decided that he liked power more than heroics.
13) True
14) True—although each member has their own archenemies, as a team, it is Darkseid.

15) True—the Joker is right at home in a twisted version of a Funhouse.
16) True—on this occasion he has teamed up with Killer Frost.
17) False—it is Terra, his former girlfriend and fellow Teen Titan who betrays the team.
18) False—it is the evil Cyborg Superman that Supergirl has often fought.
19) True—although they used to be friends, Jor-El had to imprison Zod in the Phantom Zone.

20) False—his name is Gentleman Ghost.
21) True
22) True
23) True—while The Flash might see Reverse-Flash as the greater threat, Captain Cold would disagree!
24) False—it is another chilly villain, Killer Frost.
25) False—it is his father Darkseid's servant Desaad.
26) True—Catwoman draws the line at some of Black Mask's

evil deeds.
27) False—it is Lady Shiva.
28) False—Two-Face has clashed most with Batman's various sidekicks.
29) True—but Batman is more than equipped to see off his archenemy!
30) False—he has to build high-tech battle suits even to have a chance against the Man of Steel.

PAGES 64-65
VILLAINS' LAIRS

1) False—he doesn't have one regular base, although his hideouts are often called the Ha-Hacienda.
2) c. Iceberg Lounge
3) a. A nightclub
4) True—of course!

5) b. Swinging ax
6) c. Cube
7) a. They lose their powers
8) d. 96 stories
9) b. Not enough parking spaces
10) c. 6
11) d. The Phantom Zone

12) c. Africa
13) b. Apokolips
14) c. The sewers
15) a. Gotham City
16) b. Stay out!
Genius Question: The planet Korugar

AGES 66-67
LEX LUTHOR

1) c. Wonder Woman
2) c. Black and green
3) d. Orange
4) d. Metropolis
5) True
6) b. The Legion of Doom
7) True—until Batman and Superman expose him as

corrupt.
8) c. Black Manta and Sinestro
9) b. Purple and green
10) b. Deathstroke
11) d. Martian Manhunter
12) c. The Joker
13) a. His mind
14) a. Helicopter

15) c. Green Kryptonite
16) False—Lex believes he always does what's best for Earth, even if his methods can be brutal.
Genius Question: Lena Luthor

PAGES 68-69
EVIL GADGETS AND TECHNOLOGY

1) b. Kryptonite gun
2) b. To slow down The Flash
3) a. Deconstructor
4) d. Batarangs
5) c. Giant boxing glove
6) b. Ice prison

7) d. Cream pie boomerang
8) d. Detonator
9) a. Sea Saucer
10) c. Cannonball shooter
11) b. Shrinking
12) a. Fear gas tank

13) d. All of the above
14) b. Scarface
15) c. Laughing gas missile
16) True—it was the LexCorp duplicator ray.
Genius Question: Killer Moth

AGES 70-71
EPIC BATTLES

1) False—it is three, but they are no match for Superman when he is in fighting mood!
2) False—for a battle against a flying villain, Batman takes to the skies in the Batcopter.
3) False—it is Superman that he is ready to battle.

4) True—using the yellow light of fear he has constructed a power staff.
5) True—they are Superman, Cyborg, Hawkman, and Green Arrow.
6) False—it is Cyborg who is left behind, but he is saved

by the Martian Manhunter.
7) True—alien Brainiac faces off against fellow aliens Supergirl, Superman, and Martian Manhunter.
8) False—although one battle is against Catwoman, the other is Killer Moth.

9) False—it is Captain Cold.
10) True
11) True—though it may not be enough to defeat Batman in battle.
12) True—the formation of the Justice League had given the bad guys no chance of winning.
13) True
14) False—it was all a dream!
15) False—the Bizarros battle against Darkseid's forces.
16) False—it is General Zod.
17) True—the mischievous imp captured the rest of the League to lure Batman to him.
18) True—but the battle was just a distraction for Lex Luthor and Darkseid's real mission!

19) False—they use Black Manta's ship, which Lex says "smells like a wharf."
20) True—one of his hands is missing and has been replaced by a hook!
21) False—they are fighting off the Parademons with Plasma Guns.
22) True—the Apokoliptian bad guys are trying to steal a Mother Box.
23) False—Blue Beetle, not Superman, is the flying hero in the set.
24) True—Batman used a concentrated blast of yellow sun rays to break Brainiac's control.
25) False—he tried this plan,

but in the end Robin's suggestion of a heartfelt speech worked instead.
26) True
27) True—but Batman saves the day by getting inside his head to turn his shrink ray into a growth ray.
28) False—it is Lex Luthor.
29) False—he teams up with the Justice League to battle Brainiac and help save the Earth.
30) True

PAGES 72-73
INFAMOUS HEISTS

1) d. Dr. Harleen Quinzel
2) a. Duck
3) c. Endangered birds
4) a. In his umbrella's handle
5) b. Diamonds
6) d. Crime-of-the-Month Club
7) b. The Rogues

8) d. Heat Wave
9) c. Antique violins
10) a. Presenting a basement-based TV prank show
11) b. Fish
12) d. A bank
13) b. Poison Ivy

14) True—but the thieves were foiled by Vicki Vale.
15) d. Diamonds
16) b. Maid
17) a. The Penguin

PAGES 74-75
KINGS OF THE UNDERWORLD

1) a. Motorcycle
2) b. Diamonds
3) False—the marks next to the bat-symbol show how often the Penguin has failed to beat Batman.
4) a. A fish and an umbrella
5) d. Mask

6) c. Freeze gun
7) d. Heat Wave
8) False—he wears a monocle.
9) d. Talia, his daughter
10) c. Sword
11) True—he underwent training after being bullied as a child.

12) a. The Demon's Head
13) b. Oswald Cobblepot
14) b. Tan
15) a. Ice cream
16) b. Ketchup and mustard
Genius Question: Venom

PAGES 76-77
THE JOKER

1) False—probably! Nobody knows the Joker's true identity, not even Batman.
2) True—she was his psychiatrist!
3) True—he does love to look at himself!
4) True—looking after Gotham City for Batman, Superman found out just how much trouble the Joker was!
5) False—he has caught Robin, tying him up over a barrel of fish.
6) True—it's a trick gun, of course!

7) False—he tends to have green hair.
8) True—you never know what sneaky tricks he will try!
9) True—he also holds the record for escapes!
10) True—in those, days Red Hood was a criminal, but now Jason Todd has made him a hero.
11) False—he has a cream pie.
12) True—the first time he looks at his reflection, he goes crazy!
13) True—he drew a face on it and called it Spoony!
14) True—he knows that it is

vital to take the Joker seriously.
15) False—it is the Clown Prince of Crime.
16) False—it is a runaway roller-coaster wagon.
17) False—he has no superpowers, just a knack for mayhem and practical jokes!
18) True—well, Joker wasn't going to win it fair and square!

19) True—until Batman caught up with his evil ice cream truck.
20) True—it's one of his favorite weapons.
21) True—its bouncing suspension makes it impossible for Gothamites to ignore.
22) False—the pair try, but the Joker can't stand working with Scarecrow.

23) False—he is an expert chemist and formulates his own potions.
24) True—whether they like it or not!
25) False—it's a Batman dummy, naturally!
26) False—it's a chicken.
27) True—it will squirt out water or unpleasant chemicals.

28) False—unless your idea of fun is getting a big electric shock!
29) False—Ivy hates the Joker for not being nicer to her friend Harley Quinn.
30) True—although he eventually decided it was too corny, even for him!

PAGES 78-79
JOKERLAND

1) a. Wheels of Fire
2) b. Robin
3) True—in 6864 Batman and the Two-Face Chase and 7781 The Batmobile: Two-Face's Escape.

4) False—there are three sets.
5) c. Two
6) d. Delicious
7) c. Starfire
8) False—Poison Ivy is holding a

long vine whip.
9) b. Poison
10) False—he only has one.

PAGES 80-81
VILLAINOUS VEHICLES

1) a. A manta ray
2) b. On a hover platform
3) c. Harley Quinn
4) b. Battle Chomper
5) True
6) a. A dragster

7) d. A giant smile
8) c. Purple
9) b. A roller coaster car
10) a. Laughing gas
11) c. Black Zero
12) c. Killer Frost

13) d. Space Hog
14) True—it can spring out to punch pursuers.
15) c. Bane
16) a. Jet ski
Genius Question: Tentacles

PAGES 82-83
CATWOMAN

1) d. Selina Kyle
2) c. Purple
3) True—Robin was not impressed!
4) c. Gotham City
5) b. Princess of Plunder
6) b. Milk

7) d. All of the above
8) a. Cat o'nine tails whip
9) d. Poison Ivy and Harley Quinn
10) b. Goggles
11) a. Motorcycle
12) True

13) c. A tail
14) b. A diamond
15) a. Clawed gloves
16) True—but she finds it hard to keep on the right side of the law for long!
Genius Question: Isis

PAGES 84-85
BAD BEASTS

1) False—Grodd is trying to steal a crate of them!
2) c. Dynamite
3) d. Killer Moth
4) a. Gorilla Grodd
5) d. King Shark
6) True

7) a. Barbara Minerva
8) c. Cat
9) b. Captain Boomerang
10) c. Waylon Jones
11) a. Using an untested serum
12) a. Blue
13) c. It's a genetic condition

14) d. Gorilla City
15) False—it is Wonder Woman.
16) a. Telepathy
Genius Question: Zebra-Man

PAGES 88-89
GOTHAM CITY

1) True
2) False—it is Blackgate Penitentiary.
3) True—though they often escape!
4) False—it is Crime Alley.
5) False—he gives

Superman the job.
6) True
7) False—he comes from Slaughter Swamp.
8) False—it was the Ace Chemical Processing Plant.

9) False—it is on the outskirts of the city.
10) True—the Waynes and the Kanes feuded for generations.
11) True

12) True—after a natural disaster, she closed the park off to everyone except children.
13) False—it is the Diamond District.
14) True
15) False—there are 13 guardians.
16) True
17) True
18) True—her name is Mayor McCaskill.
19) False—it is called Amusement Mile.
20) False—she hails from the rundown East End.
21) False—both were expelled.
22) True
23) True
24) True
25) False—he knows that there are plenty of bad cops there!
26) True—he finds it too gloomy!
27) True
28) True
29) False—Gotham's is called the Statue of Justice.
30) True

PAGES 90–91
METROPOLIS

1) b. The Big Apricot
2) d. Lextown
3) c. The *Daily Planet*
4) c. The Avenue of Tomorrow
5) c. Superman and General Zod
6) d. Scientific research
7) b. Lois Lane
8) b. The Hall of Justice
9) c. A car
10) d. Blaze Comics
11) d. Four
12) b. Trapping him under an antenna tower
13) b. Metropolis University
14) d. Lex Luthor
15) a. The LexCorp Tower
16) b. Brainiac
17) a. Teen Titans

PAGES 92–93
KRYPTON

1) False—Krypton's sun is red.
2) True
3) False—He is from the city of Kryptonopolis.
4) False—they are scientists.
5) True
6) False—Kryptonians only have powers while on Earth.
7) False—Lois does not feature in this set.
8) True
9) False—Kryptonians get their powers from Earth's yellow sun.
10) False—Zod knew Superman's father, but he is no relation.
11) True—General Zod, Tor-An, Faora and of course, Superman!
12) True
13) False—Kryptonite is created when the planet explodes.
14) False—it has two separate species called the metal-eating mole and the thought beast.
15) True—Doomsday was created in a Kryptonian lab.
16) False—it exploded in the year 10,000.
17) True—she only appears in the LEGO Brainiac Attack set.
18) True
19) True—Kryptonite is one of the few things that makes Superman weak.
20) True—the light from the explosion takes 27 years to reach Earth.
21) False—his father is called Jor-El. Zor-El is Superman's uncle.
22) True
23) False—it has four.
24) False—there are seven other planets in Krypton's solar system.
25) True—Superman's dog Krypto is one.
26) True—it projects its thoughts onto the screen.
27) True
28) False—it is home to some of the most dangerous creatures in the universe.
29) True—they wear the armor to breathe while they adapt to Earth's atmosphere.
30) False—he wears black armor
31) False—but they can extend their lives with cloned body parts.
32) True—he puts the city in a bottle just before the planet explodes.

PAGES 94–95
AROUND THE WORLD

1) d. Australia
2) c. U.K.
3) a. Vixen
4) c. Arctic
5) b. Blue
6) a. Mexico
7) c. China
8) b. Switzerland
9) b. Nottingham
10) False—Black Lightning protects Los Angeles.
11) True—he has a large design of the U.K.'s flag on his chest.
12) a. Seattle
13) b. The Caribbean Sea
14) d. Africa
15) b. London
16) c. Philadelphia
Genius Question: Quebec

FAMILY

1) b. Komand'r
2) True—both are called Martha.
3) c. Cousin
4) b. Alfred
5) d. Jor-El
6) b. Commissioner Gordon
7) c. Talia

8) a. Aquaman
9) b. Batwoman
10) c. Mother
11) c. Zan
12) True—the rivals agreed to swap their sons to ensure peace between them.

13) a. Kalibak
14) True—although the one exception is Lightning Lad's older brother.
15) d. No relation
16) b. Raven
Genius Question: His father, Silas Stone.

PAGES 98-99
ANIMALS

1) b. Krypton
2) c. Streaky
3) c. Titus
4) c. Scorpion
5) b. Ace the Bat-Hound
6) a. Utility Collar
7) True

8) a. Cat
9) d. Bat-Cow
10) c. Wonder Dog
11) a. Monkey
12) b. Ultra-Humanite
13) True—Thomas Blake is a hunter who turns to crime after

losing his fortune.
14) d. Turtle
15) b. Dex-Starr
16) True—he can change into any animal, even a prehistoric one!
Genius Question: A duck called Duck Dodgers!

ALIEN WORLDS

1) False—her secret island home is found on Earth.
2) True—they protect them from the dangerous metallic animals that live there, too!
3) False—she is from Titan, a moon orbiting Saturn.
4) True
5) False—she is from Tamaran.
6) True—but they do not share her other powers.
7) False—Hal Jordan is a normal human being.
8) True—natives of Korugar all have purple skin, like Sinestro.
9) False—it was made by the Weaponers of an opposite-universe world called Qward.

10) False—it is Nok.
11) False—Colonel Hardy is the human backup for Superman.
12) False—Black Manta is a human from Earth.
13) True
14) True
15) False—Coluans are green.
16) True—tricksy Mr. Mxyzptlk also comes from this dimension.
17) True—it is Doomsday.
18) True—he was cloned in a lab.
19) True—he is Darkseid's uncle.
20) True
21) False—Nth Metal comes from Thanagar.
22) True—it is a horrible place!
23) False—but the Justice

League have battled Starro, a giant starfish-like alien.
24) True
25) True
26) False—he loves chocolate cookies!
27) True—but he now roams space as a bounty hunter.
28) False—the lack of people on his planet is down to Lobo.
29) False—they are brother and sister.
30) True—Zan can become anything from a monsoon to a frost giant!

PAGES 102-103
ROMANCE

1) b. Lois Lane
2) c. Steve Trevor
3) a. Puddin'
4) c. Green Arrow
5) d. Talia al Ghūl
6) b. Nora
7) c. Spoiler
8) True—she starts dating Hal when

he is a test pilot for her Ferris Aircraft company.
9) d. Mera
10) b. Beast Boy
11) False—they have occasionally been a couple.
12) a. Lightning Lad
13) b. Barbara Gordon

14) c. Beast Boy
15) True—they are destined to be together!
16) b. Lana Lang
Genius Question: She broke him out of prison so they could commit crazy crimes!

PAGES 104-105
CAREERS

1) b. Newspaper reporter
2) a. Crime laboratory
3) c. Actor
4) d. Wrestler

5) a. Pilot
6) True—he was a stage actor; his makeup skills are useful if Master Bruce needs a disguise!

7) d. Botanist
8) a. Psychiatrist
9) d. The Joker
10) a. Two-Face

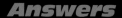

11) a. Drill sergeant
12) c. Leonard Snart
(Captain Cold)

13) False—he was a special-effects expert in Hollywood.
14) a. Nightwing

15) c. Lois Lane
16) b. Black Canary
Genius Question: Zatanna

PAGES 106–107
ROBOTS

1) a. Cyborg
2) d. Cybots
3) b. Superman
4) c. A net shooter
5) True—they may look cute, but his robots are trouble!
6) d. Doomsday

7) True—until a malfunction made him go bad. Now he shrinks planets and puts them in jars!
8) a. Toyman
9) b. Dynamite
10) d. 25th
11) b. Shark

12) b. Laser shooters
13) c. Red Tornado
14) c. Kryptonite
15) True—it is powered by a small rocket booster.
16) c. Green
Genius Question: Metallo

PAGES 108–109
ATLANTIS

1) False—the razor-sharp wings can also be used as weapons.
2) True—all the better to steal the Mother Box with!

3) b. Flying Fox: Batmobile Airlift Attack
4) c. Poison Ivy
5) True
6) b. Two

7) True—after it sank, the Atlanteans adapted to life beneath the sea.
8) a. Trident
9) b. Steppenwolf

PAGES 110–111
CLONES AND DISGUISES

1) d. Superman and Lex Luthor
2) c. Project Cadmus
3) d. Lex Luthor
4) a. Kon-El
5) b. Superman
6) b. The Joker
7) c. Giant fists
8) d. Assisting in a laboratory

9) d. Purple
10) b. Charles Szasz
11) c. John Jones
12) a. Matches Malone
13) b. The World's Worst Detective
14) a. An old lady
15) True—but he can't maintain the shape for very long.

16) True—by slumping his shoulders to appear shorter and meeker, Clark has almost everyone fooled!
Genius Question: Plastic Man

PAGES 112–113
TIME TRAVEL AND MIND CONTROL

1) d. The Flash
2) c. The Batcave
3) b. Cavemen times
4) a. Pirate
5) d. Booster Gold
6) False—super-villain Doctor Destiny is a mind-controller; he makes nightmares become real!

7) d. A flute
8) a. Kid Flash
9) True
10) False—Martian Manhunter is famous for mind-control powers.
11) a. Cyborg
12) c. Mad Hatter

13) b. Legion of Super-Heroes
14) c. Riddler
15) b. Brainiac
16) a. His helmet
Genius Question: Saturn Girl

PAGES 114–115
MYSTERIOUS ARTIFACTS

1) d. Bathing in a Lazarus Pit
2) b. Hephaestus
3) a. His helmet
4) b. Bane
5) a. Lasso of Truth
6) c. Soultaker
7) d. 600 years

8) a. Trident of Poseidon
9) c. Mother Box
10) d. A sentient computer
11) b. The planet New Genesis
12) c. Boom tubes
13) True—the Father Box draws its power from negative

forces in the universe.
14) a. Cyborg
15) d. All of the above
16) False—the Central Power Battery on Oa powers the rings of all Green Lanterns.
Genius Question: Blue

Editor Rosie Peet
Senior Editor Alastair Dougall
Editorial Assistant Hannah Gulliver-Jones
Project Art Editor Rhys Thomas
Designers Sam Bartlett, James McKeag, and Lisa Sodeau
Pre-Production Producer Siu Chan
Producer Lloyd Robertson
Managing Editor Paula Regan
Managing Art Editor Jo Connor
Art Director Lisa Lanzarini
Publisher Julie Ferris
Publishing Director Simon Beecroft

Written by Melanie Scott

First American Edition, 2018
Published in the United States by DK Publishing
345 Hudson Street, New York, New York 10014

Page design copyright ©2018 Dorling Kindersley Limited
DK, a Division of Penguin Random House LLC
18 19 20 21 22 10 9 8 7 6 5 4 3 2 1
001–305845–July/18

Published in Great Britain by Dorling Kindersley Limited.

A catalog record for this book is available
from the Library of Congress.

ISBN: 978-1-46546-757-7

DK books are available at special discounts when purchased in bulk for sales
promotions, premiums, fund-raising, or educational use. For details, contact:
DK Publishing Special Markets, 345 Hudson Street, New York, New York 10014
SpecialSales@dk.com

Printed and bound in China

A WORLD OF IDEAS:
SEE ALL THERE IS TO KNOW

www.LEGO.com
www.dk.com